Carolyn Westbrook

THROUGH
THE FRENCH DOOR

Carolyn Westbrook

THROUGH
THE FRENCH DOOR

Romantic interiors inspired by classic French style

PHOTOGRAPHY BY KEITH SCOTT MORTON

CICO BOOKS
LONDON NEW YORK

Published in 2012 by CICO Books
An imprint of
Ryland Peters & Small Ltd
519 Broadway, 5th floor, New York NY 10012
20–21 Jockey's Fields, London WC1R 4BW

www.cicobooks.com

10 9 8 7 6 5 4 3 2 1

A CIP catalog record for this book is available from
the Library of Congress and the British Library.

ISBN 978 1 908170 79 8

Printed in China

Managing Editor: Gillian Haslam
Editor: Helen Ridge
Designer: Christine Wood
Photographer: Keith Scott Morton

For digital editions visit www.cicobooks.com/apps.php

Contents

Introduction

Welcome home and welcome back to the historic plantation house that I call home. It is my pleasure to invite you once again to share my love of beautiful French-inspired interiors in my latest book, *Through the French Door*. As you all know, I have a continuing romance with this enormous plantation house with its 53 acres that stands in the middle of nowhere. When we bought it, it was in a state of complete disrepair—the paint was peeling and the roof was sagging—and we really needed vision to recognize its potential and bring it back to life. Before we moved in, I often used to drive out to gaze at it and wonder if it would ever feel like home. Now I cannot imagine living anywhere else.

"Creating a Home that Reflects the Spirit of You" has been my mantra since the beginning. There is nothing more pleasing than turning a house into a home that tells your story. Everyone's home should be as different as their personality and their history. In that way, those who visit can feel your embrace as they walk through the door.

I believe that your home should envelop you in beauty, familiarity, and comfort, like open arms welcoming you home at the end of the day. Lately, I have been traveling back and forth to New York, which has been exciting—I do love the inspiration and fast pace of the city—but when it is time to come home, I cannot wait to be back. Sometimes on the perfect day, I find myself lying across my bed, with its puffy feather and satin eiderdown, with my piles of magazines and the dogs close by, while my teenage children shout from the other room, "What's for dinner?", and I know that I am home.

Join us, then, in this beautifully photographed book as we revel in the eclectic and personal interiors that have evolved from carefully picked possessions, reminding us of somewhere, something, or someone that we love. Life goes by in the blink of an eye, and it seems just yesterday my kids were small and dreaming of Santa. Home is all about such memories, so take good care of it and dress it well.

Roam through the halls of a Big City House with us, and be inspired by the simple, sleek decoration of a Town and Country interior. Experience for yourself what true French Country Living looks like, and peer into our rustic Fisherman's Cabin.

RIGHT *Like the plantation house, the potting shed was in a state of great disrepair when we bought it. We had to rebuild the porch and add shutters to the front of the building. Now the zinc-topped table is always in use for repotting plants and coddling seedlings. Even though it is just a potting shed, there are many elements here that reflect our personalities, interests, and history, from the bee skep atop a classical column to the antique organza curtains at the windows.*

LEFT A lampshade reflects the same colors and patterns as the vintage handmade screen behind it.

RIGHT A stack of wonderful antique red books that hold stories of classic literature look marvelous stacked beneath this exquisite bird bowl that once belonged to my grandmother and now houses the Shamrock plant.

We share with you our return to the farmhouse life that we revel in here at the plantation. In the marketing world, the farm lifestyle has become big news—something made in, and for, Hollywood—but for us it is the life that we actually lead. It is completely genuine and has been for years. We make the trek out to the hen house every morning to gather eggs and pick tomatoes from the garden, but that is just one aspect of farmhouse life, and I happen to adore them all.

Our plantation house is ever-changing, and since refreshing, redecorating, and remodeling are my passion, this home is always a work in progress, and that goes for the grounds as well—we are constantly redoing the porches, the garden house, and even the chicken coop.

You must not miss the seasonal celebrations of the year. You are an honored guest, and we welcome you with true southern hospitality. Everyone who knows me knows how I love to throw a party, and I am quite thrilled to be able to share some of the events and celebrations that go on here, from an outdoor spring gathering to a Christmas celebration. It is always a good time for a party… am I right? So, make yourself comfortable as I invite you *Through the French Door*. Welcome home, my friend.

xo Carolyn

chapter one

Inspired Interiors

• Welcome Home • For the Love of Pink • French Country Living
• Big City House • Town and Country • Black and White
• The Making of a Collection

Welcome Home

Once again, I would like to welcome you to the plantation that my family and I call home. It is where my passion

lies, and it continues to be a work in progress that is forever evolving as the years pass by, just like me. I think back

to my childhood and how that family home would also change through the seasons and over the course of time.

Whatever my mother was passionate about, she reflected it in our home. Her interior design choices were far-

reaching, from modern and sleek to Asian-themed, but regardless of the style, our home was always comfortable

and beautiful. The things that she loved most and couldn't bear to part with were constant features. Such elements form the base of every design plan, and around them you can style your entire home.

The photograph below shows the entrance to our plantation home. It makes a grand impression on all who visit but, above all, it is welcoming. In it are pieces that have been carefully selected over the years and have special significance. They have been brought together here for a fantastic result.

BELOW *First impressions matter, which means that the entrance to every home is so very important. Various pieces of furniture, of different styles and periods, come together to create a space that is warm and inviting. The weeping palm and white hydrangeas extend the welcome even further.*

Well-considered, layered displays bring much interest to a room

Just inside the door, you will find an old mirror, with all of its imperfections, from an old Odd Fellows Lodge in Nebraska. A layered collection of three different sizes of antique brown transferware platters that seem to look perfect on the wall set the backdrop for an old oil painting that came from the French flea markets. A weeping palm adds the live element that is so essential to any room, and a mix of chairs from different periods and of varied sizes makes a very large space suddenly seem warm and welcoming.

LEFT *A ghost mirror with all of its imperfections makes it more about the decoration than for peering into and forms a backdrop to a collection that somehow seems to fit together nicely.*

RIGHT *These straw-like suitcases are quite collectable and have a history all their own. Fitting the space perfectly, they are also practical, concealing those items that are best not left on show. An eclectic mix of armchairs makes the room appear less formal, and the plump cushions ensure that visitors are seated in style and comfort.*

There is so much more to creating a home than going to a furniture store and randomly choosing a packaged room. As I always say, your home should tell the story of everyone who dwells there. We have all made different journeys through life, and our homes should speak out about where we have been, whom we have met, and who is dear to us. It should show off those special trinkets and trappings that we have picked up along the way.

Many of you will be faced with a blank canvas, and all those white walls and empty spaces needing to be filled can seem a daunting task. In such a situation, it is often a good idea to break the space down into smaller vignettes, which seem to warm up a room and make it more intimate and comfortable. This is what I have done here. I have created a small seating area in a large entrance hall and deliberately chosen a random assortment of French chairs and benches, to create a more relaxed feel. Gorgeous oil paintings and diverse collections create a layered effect and make the room breathtaking and interesting, all at the same time. Most importantly, they are telling a story.

LEFT An assortment of framed paintings and prints turns a plain painted wall into an amazing focal point.

BELOW LEFT I found this entire collection of liquor decanter bottles, packed in a cardboard box, at a flea market in the middle of a field. Scrubbed clean and refilled, they now provide refreshment for visitors.

BELOW A stack of plain vanilla-colored books never looked so good, complementing the occasional table on which they are displayed. The elegant metal dog on top was made many years ago in Germany.

Layer, layer, layer…that is my belief and this place has reflected this to perfection. From the old velvet theater drapes that are the backdrop behind the bed to the stunning old mirror that is crumbling in all of the right places and looks magnificent as the focal point of the room. The mirror brings the "wow" factor to this room and it serves as the most glorious headboard of sorts and an original approach to the question of what kind of headboard to use. Unexpected elements in a room are always welcome, and the Asian hand-painted black screen fulfills this role particularly well. It is also an integral part of the background in the layering process.

LEFT *Filled with wonderful objects of special significance, this sumptuous and extravagant bedroom is for me the epitome of a sanctuary.*

BELOW *A collection of wicker bottles and beautifully detailed ornaments of a ewe and her lamb make a highly individual layered display on the bedside table.*

Full-blown antique roses that reveal ruffled petals tinged in pink are not only the most beautiful blooms, but also give off a decadent scent, while candles glow in the crystal rose bowls. This bedroom is truly a sanctuary and no detail has been overlooked, from the way it smells to the way it feels when one climbs into the puffed featherbed. The linen duvet and bedspread create the ultimate top-of-bed dressing.

Another of my passions is the detail in the magnificent animals that I so love to collect. Most of the old ones come from Germany, as they seem to be the masters at the beautifully detailed faces of the farm animals, as well as the metal deer that are a passion of mine. If I see these out and about, it seems that I simply cannot resist having them. I usually tell myself that I am buying them for resell, but they never seem to make it that far. Somehow, they always end up canoodling with the other ones that I have collected!

RIGHT *A bed that is layered in gorgeous linens, a table draped in a printed silk, and a room that offers both comfort and beauty.*

LEFT *The seductive scent of antique roses, displayed in cut crystal bowls, permeates the air. Candles alongside add to the romance.*

BELOW *An even closer glimpse and we can see the essence of this collection and the great texture and carefully compiled sizes of these coveted wicker bottles presented on an old silver pedestal plateau.*

For the Love of Pink

Pink was a passion of mine when I was young, as it is for most girls, and it has remained my favorite color ever since. I do venture out and try all sorts of colors and combinations, and have often stayed away from pink for fear of using it too much. Sometimes a love for another color will arise but my romance with pink endures. I believe most women share my passion, although many will not admit to it, thinking it is too childlike, or they may fear that the men in their lives won't approve. I, on the other hand, consider pink to be a neutral color, and one that goes with practically anything.

In this bedroom, pink prevails but doesn't overwhelm. Flowers and a paisley pattern in subtle pinks and creams mingle together on the bed linen. Barely cream walls and simple white linen drapes surround the iron-framed bed, which is the centerpiece of the room. The beautiful trees just outside the French door and balcony add their own beauty to this backdrop and beckon you outside. Oil paintings, precious rugs, and my cherished Italian tole table, all come together to create a look that is breathtaking.

As I redecorate, I move my favorite pieces from room to room, and end up creating somewhere altogether new. The old faded pink concrete swan was meant for a garden but it now overlooks the head of the bed. Festooned with fresh greenery, it brings something unexpected to the space. A French urn on a gilded French pedestal, meanwhile, adds just the right note of sophistication and luster. I particularly love the palest pastel pink in the Italian tole table. This treasured piece was found while en route to Atlanta. Wherever it is placed in the house, it is always inspiring. Now, it is just perfect perched at the end of the bed and alongside the armchair covered in pink toile de Jouy.

LEFT *This bedroom is the stuff that dreams are made of—soothing, romantic, and undeniably pretty in pink.*

RIGHT *Books with pale pink bindings look beautiful used as a riser for the crystal rose bowl of vivid pink blooms.*

LEFT *The love affair with pink continues with the barely blush roses and an antique Venetian mirror trimmed in pink. Reflected in the mirror are a decanter etched with ferns and a matching glass bottle.*

RIGHT *Pink books, pink roses, and a pink-edged mirror inject subtle color into this romantic desktop display. The two mirrors and the ornate table lamp with a handmade pleated linen shade add to the layered effect.*

Not only is this pink space French inspired but it also speaks of the beauty of vintage pieces and romance. The bright pink chest takes center stage in this vignette, flanked by simple white French chairs. A fabulous gilded mirror hangs above. Fitting in perfectly are an oversized vintage floral lampshade and an urn of vivid pink hydrangeas, either side of the antique oil painting. All these pieces were found at different times and at different places, but they all work together to create just the right look.

LEFT *This close-up of the antique oil painting on the chest leaves you in no doubt that it is the "cherry on top" in this vignette. Leading the eye to this Parisian flea-market find are vivid pink hydrangeas and a lamp with a vintage floral lampshade.*

RIGHT *Simple white French chairs flank the chest and a gorgeous old oil painting from the Paris flea markets tops off the space beautifully.*

Whatever the room, it should always contain a living element. In this bedroom, the outside is brought in with an antique garden urn atop a gorgeous gilded pedestal, while a topiary adorned with pink blooms is the crowning glory. Floral motifs, especially roses, can be relied upon to bring beauty and romance to a room, whether they are the flowers of an antique rose, a painted motif on porcelain, or the pattern of an antique rug.

This rug, a long-time favorite of mine, has graced the floors all around our house. It is threadbare in places and faded from catching the sun's rays through the windows, but it is this gently aged beauty that makes it all the more special to me. My interiors are all about time-worn beauty but it takes perseverance to collect. I could never buy a replacement rug of this age and with this patina in a department store.

BELOW, BELOW LEFT, AND RIGHT
Flowers entwine on the threadbare and faded rug, delicate floral sprigs adorn the china teapot, and a topiary wreath is topped with pink blooms. All these elements come together in a spectacular vignette inspired by nature.

This mantel is the ultimate in layering. A pile of mirrors and frames that were in separate places are put together and look beautiful. I always find decorating mantels a bit tricky. I don't like them to look too contrived, but this one seemed to naturally come together. One of my favorite prints was wasting away in a bathroom so I brought it in to be enjoyed, and a figurine of a lounging woman seemed like the perfect pairing to the old print. An old concrete Venus statue completed the look and it all turned out to be a beautiful and cohesive collection. Just outside in the hallway is a petite French console table that sits beneath a small pink alabaster lamp that is a favorite, while a pretty mirror reflects a white linen bed.

RIGHT *An all-white setting in the hall is infused with a pretty injection of pink with the petite alabaster lamp, roses, and vintage garden print.*

BELOW LEFT AND BELOW *A mantel in one of the upstairs bedrooms becomes an interesting vignette.*

French Country Living

French Country Living, as exemplified here, is all about relaxing in time-worn comfort. Everything in the room has been very carefully chosen, which takes years of collecting the right ingredients. Beautiful pieces of furniture in the living area have been arranged in a way that is inviting and comfortable. There is no hint of pretension or stuffiness, which is what I love about this style of decoration.

On entering the room, you simply want to head straight for the couch and plop yourself down, to be enveloped by the down-filled pillows. If the couch is already taken, there is plenty of alternative seating to be had. The windows, too, are welcoming, dressed up with elegant drapes in warm neutral hues, while the lighting, soft and balanced, has been designed to perfection. Due care and attention has also been given to the placement of paintings and shelves. Many people have a tendency to hang small pieces of art on a large wall so they are dwarfed, or they hang them too high so they can't be appreciated. The artworks here are masterfully placed, as shown by the painting hung low by the corner table, counterbalanced by the adjacent cupboard.

LEFT *Beautiful surroundings, plenty of comfortable seating, and treasured pieces, such as the bamboo shelving in the corner, make this the perfect living area.*

RIGHT *In a kitchen corner, antique breadboards are stacked to provide a platform for a vintage Italian cow.*

The French Country Living style prevails in this living room, where an inviting fireplace anchors the space and beckons all to gather. The soaring ceilings expand the size of the room, but it remains cozy with all the interesting and comfortable surroundings.

Lighting sets the tone of any room. Overhead lighting alone makes a room appear cold and uninviting. Atmosphere and warmth are created here through pretty table lamps in a range of sizes, scattered around the room—the prettier they are, the better.

A priority for any interior is great oil paintings. By that, I don't mean expensive paintings by the masters, just ones that speak to you—you will know them when you see them. The only good art I've ever found is vintage. This means hitting the flea markets, antique malls, and garage sales. But you can make a room interesting with more than just artwork—a gorgeous collection of plates, platters, and lids graces these walls. Plants, too, bring color and interest, even more so when they are in unusual containers.

With my layered style of living, the throw or eiderdown is ever present. It not only brings in more pattern and texture, but softens a room when thrown over a couch or chair, creating a partnership of comfort and beauty.

ABOVE *Rugs are a necessity, as is comfortable seating, for a living room. An enormous and fabulous painting, bought at a late-night auction, becomes the focal point of this wall.*

RIGHT *In spite of the soaring ceiling, this room appears cozy and intimate, thanks in part to the warm, neutral color palette of the furniture and decoration.*

In my last book, *The French Inspired Home*, I had a chapter focusing on French Bleu. Blue is dramatic and can be portrayed in so many variations from cobalt blue to the palest French blue that is reminiscent of the Asiatic Pheasant transferware that I collect. I seem to be attracted to them all.

Here a marvelous blue antique sink has been reborn into this little hallway powder room and placing it inside this marble-topped washstand turns an ordinary room into one that demands a second look. Meanwhile, in the dining room, my treasured collection of blue transferware forms part of a delightful blue and oatmeal collage with a pine buffet. The buffet had been waiting in our barn for twelve years for a place in our home. I have always loved pine and it suddenly struck me that it would look wonderful

BELOW LEFT *A blue antique china sink, inserted into a marble-topped washstand, is undeniably the focal point in this powder room.*

BELOW *The pale French blue toile panels highlight the transferware plates in front beautifully. Their different shades of blue look gorgeous with the pine buffet.*

BELOW *Generous drapes of deep blue bring drama to this hushed bedroom of dark wood. The bamboo shade, pulled down part of the way, frames the concrete statue of a woman outside, drawing our eye toward her.*

here and also provide much needed storage. The arched doors make it a striking piece, and its rich, warm color shows off the transferware to perfection. It goes to show that if you have a piece that you love, never let it go. Take a step back and think about where it would work best in your home. This single piece has given a whole new look to a room badly in need of redecoration. It made me wonder why I hadn't done it before but even designers become complacent about refreshing their homes.

The bedroom here is simply and quietly gorgeous. The mahogany dresser grounds the room, while the blue print drapes add a sense of drama, at the same time softening the dark wood elements. A wonderful antique "puff" beckons one to snuggle up and have a contented nap.

This bedroom celebrates my love of layering

This is a bedroom that reminds one of coming home. It has a French Country appeal with French ticking and red accents that make for a charming room. A chair is upholstered in antique French fabrics with the red embroidered laundry monograms. I learned while in France that the initials that are found on antique French textiles actually are to identify items when sent to the laundry—another great detail to be cherished and displayed years later.

A great display of how to decorate a wall becomes evident here, and the focal point is a family antique crazy quilt. This collage is carefully composed of antique antlers and ancestor photos that have been arranged to perfection. Red accents are reflected in the lamps, baskets, and bedding. This room celebrates my love of layering and remembering my motto, more is more.

LEFT *The rich, red, toile wallpaper flows everywhere in this room, and includes the ceiling, encouraging one to look up. The painting, which includes a touch of red, looks beautiful hanging with the wallpaper. The towels are accented with red embroidered initials and tie into the powder room beautifully.*

RIGHT *Twin beds are layered to perfection, starting with a dust ruffle and finishing with plump pillows covered in white slips with red stripes of varying widths. The backdrop of collectibles and memorabilia helps give this room its unique identity.*

Just off the kitchen is a gracious eating area, neutral in palette and big on style. This is the epitome of the French Country look, where elegance sits side by side rustic simplicity. As always, the detailing is crucial to the success of the decoration, from the tiny buttons running along the curtain panels to the tufting on the linen-covered dining chairs.

The room is awash in the faded patina that is most appealing to the eye. A wooden bowl of antlers makes for an interesting and textural arrangement on the pine cabinet. Behind the glass doors is more of my favored transferware, their deep blue making an eye-catching contrast with the wood. A tin bucket serves as a vase of sorts, for bunches of kale and hydrangeas that are picked from the bushes just outside. Overseeing it all is a beautiful antique chandelier hanging above the table. A pair of wall sconces in the same style add to the allure created by the twinkling light.

LEFT *In typically French country style, this dining space mixes the elegant with the rustic. Beautifully upholstered chairs and a pine farmhouse table are perfect partners, making this a welcoming and comfortable space for family and friends.*

Kitchen and breakfast areas can be the most challenging rooms for decoration because they need to be practical, but they can, and should be, just as beautiful as any other part of the house. Dusty fake plants that are stowed away on top of cabinets are never tolerable!

Antique pieces of furniture, such as shelving, are used here to house cooking essentials, from nuts and oatmeal to sugar and flour, stored and celebrated in vintage glass containers. Glass spooners are filled with silverware and grouped together for convenience. Stacked high and topped with forks, plates become part of the tabletop décor, while napkins are rolled and housed in a tall pedestal-type glass. Fresh herbs play a starring role, pretty and easily accessed for cooking, tucked into an antique ironstone creamer. Cheeses, croissants, and desserts are stored on pretty and mismatching glass and china cake plates of all sizes, then covered by glass domes and cloches originally intended for covering seedlings in the garden. This is a world of necessities that has been worked into a beautiful and functional display.

LEFT *Although simple and practical, this table display of white china plates, antique silverware, and delicious cheeses under glass domes makes guests feel most welcome. The domes, which were originally intended as cloches for protecting young plants, make elegant coverings.*

RIGHT *A vintage shelf, its peeling paint showing the passing of time, adds character to the kitchen as well as providing useful storage for various cooking essentials.*

When designing a room, I am always drawn to an eclectic look and style

The layering of exquisite pieces is the key to the success of these displays. The homeowner is a master at creating artwork collections, combining and cultivating them to perfection.

When designing a room, I always recommend going for an eclectic look—too much of any one thing is simply overwhelming. As you learn to mix and combine different elements that catch your eye, you become much like an artist yourself. I've been known to introduce Asian elements, even leopard prints, to my overriding French look. I love taking a bit of this and a bit of that, then combining them for a wonderful and intriguing result. My style is definitely not about having everything matching or symmetrical either—different shapes, sizes, heights, and styles are always a good idea, as is having odd numbers of things.

LEFT *A perfectly placed gathering of lovely objects makes this corner of the living room beautiful and significant. The curved shape of the black lacquer cabinet makes it look as though it was made for the space.*

RIGHT *A curvaceous, multicolored Venetian mirror is quite the find and, although small, is the focus of attention in this hallway vignette.*

Bedding is of great importance to any sleeping area, and bedding is what I am known for. The *Carolyn Westbrook Home* white linen sheets, pillow slips, and duvet covers on these fabulous matching twin poster beds suit the room to a tee. It is important to have both masculine and feminine elements in a room, and balance them according to the look you want. This room is predominantly masculine in style, but the dark wood of the furniture, which grounds the room, is lightened, brightened, and enhanced by the stark white linen bedding. All of my essential decorative elements can be found here, creating the ultimate sleeping quarters.

RIGHT *A pair of antique mahogany poster beds brings gravitas to this masculine-styled room, where oversized framed oil paintings of illustrious figures from the past grace the walls. With its low ceiling, the room could have appeared quite gloomy but this is offset by the crisp white bed linen and white paintwork.*

BELOW *A French monogrammed pillow makes for an exquisite accent to the bed, bringing an element of softness to the surroundings.*

An entrance hall should always be warm, inviting, and enticing, making the visitor long to see more

Big City House

Tucked away behind a perfectly manicured hedge and surrounded by beautiful landscaping is this one-of-a-kind big city house. The fact that it's no ordinary house is apparent the moment you set foot inside, onto the shiny checkerboard marble floor, and look up to see the extraordinary winding staircase that seems to go on forever. A crystal chandelier makes an awesome statement, glistening over the antique table, while the walls, painted a subdued shade of blue, are the perfect backdrop for the antique tapestry, dark wood, and marble floor. This really is a house that many dream of.

An entrance hall should always be warm, inviting, and enticing, and give a hint of what is just upstairs or around the corner, making the visitor long to see more. No matter what size it is, it needs to give the impression that you want to portray, and you do not have to break the bank to make it happen.

For me, a table is a necessity. The table here, with its central pedestal, is an antique but yours doesn't have to be. You can always make one from a round of wood or glass fixed onto some sort of base—it doesn't matter what because you can cover the table with a skirt that drapes to the floor. An arrangement of beautiful flowers or foliage on top will always make visitors feel welcome. A round skirted table is amazing with a vase of white lilies or a weeping palm in a concrete urn. Statuary brought in from outside can top an entry table along with stacks of old books or trays with trinkets and trappings that you have collected over the years. Candles, too, in various sizes and heights, in glass containers to accentuate the light, make striking centerpieces, especially at dusk when they glow so invitingly. Delicately scented candles will add to the ambience.

LEFT *Like the rest of the house, this entrance hall has been decorated with great care and attention to detail, making guests feel immediately welcome. Light floods the room from the window above the winding staircase and catches in the crystal chandelier. Reflecting it all is the checkerboard marble floor.*

OVERLEAF *Pistachio-green walls are a fitting contrasting backdrop for the dark wooden furniture and floors. Left uncovered when not in use, the highly polished dining table reflects the chandelier and candelabra. The welcome splash of pink from the orchids is echoed in the painting above the buffet.*

This formal dining room is perfection. The amazing architectural elements, which feature throughout the house and are a signature of its famous builder, offer the best possible starting point for its decoration. Classical-style niches provide a distinguished display case for the family silver and porcelain, while the elegant floral drapes hang beneath ornate plaster moldings. There is plenty of seating around the large dark wood table, for the glorious dinner parties and festive occasions that are enjoyed here. Fabrics, flowers, and colors all flow together, from the dark purple accents to the exquisite shade of green that graces the walls. No expense has been spared in the decoration, and it shows. This room in a big city house is just as you imagine it should be.

RIGHT *This big city house is tailor-made for all the social events that take place here, particularly in this grand dining room. The decoration is predominantly formal, which suits the style of the house.*

BELOW LEFT *A hallway table, originally from France, is now the base for a fantastic array of Majolica and Staffordshire china and a painted enamel container of pretty pink flowers.*

BELOW *When not being used, silver and porcelain are not hidden but instead shown off in this decorative niche.*

The parlor just outside the library is as elegant as all the other rooms in this big city house. As you approach the enormous curved stone mantelpiece, your eye is led immediately upward to the family's coat of arms that adorns the leaded window in the library.

The entire family room is meant for entertaining, which it is able to do in grand style. The room is quite enormous, as you can see from the billiard table that sits in front of the floor-to-ceiling windows. Even though small and insignificanct in its setting, it does provide hours of entertainment for guests!

LEFT *A peek into the library reveals the family coat of arms on the leaded window. Its bright blue, red, and gold heraldic devices stand out, as intended, against the neutral color palette of the furnishings.*

RIGHT *Sturdy iron chandeliers lead the eye downward from the quirky geometric-patterned ceiling to the enormous living space below. Used often for entertaining, the room is suitably filled with comfortable chairs, and a huge fireplace keeps the festivities going during winter.*

Hanging from the geometric-patterned ceiling are giant matching iron chandeliers, which bring the entire room together. In spite of their size, they look quite frilly and not at all oppressive. There is comfortable seating everywhere, with armchairs dotted here and there and back-to-back sofas. Moving around the room at well-attended parties is made easy with the aisle ways, which are purposely abundant. Keeping everyone warm during the winter months is an enormous fireplace, while in summer the French doors lining the walls can be thrown wide open onto the gorgeous patio outside, to accommodate even more people.

This living area is quite different from the previous family room in size as well as style. Painted in white and decorated in pastel shades, it has a less formal quality about it. Pale floral chintz adorns the Louis XV-style sofa and down cushions. Behind, French doors, which line the walls, lead out to the conservatory.

Magnificent chandeliers grace the ceilings throughout this big city house, and this room is no exception. My romance with antique floral oil paintings continues here, where an exquisite oil of old-fashioned pink roses just past their prime is highlighted by one of the crystal sconces. At night, they add a glistening detail to the walls.

I do love palms in any room setting. They add a graceful delicateness with their draping branches, and remind one of some exotic faraway place.

LEFT *A favored painting of an old-fashioned rose is set off to perfection with an elaborate French sconce, complete with crystal drops and neat fabric lampshades.*

RIGHT *The pale pastel colors that abound in this room make for an understated type of grandeur. Providing the living element and a touch of exoticism is a potted palm.*

French doors are the making of a great home. Many years ago, I moved into a tiny cottage of a house that had nothing really going for it except its hardwood floors. I immediately decided to add French doors. These, combined with the floors, turned that nondescript cottage into somewhere quite special.

No matter where you live or in what kind of house, the French door is the most appealing and practical way of introducing more light to your home. The French door on the left has been decorated with a fantastic antique lace window covering, which enhances its appeal still more. The covering is also hugely practical, filtering out bright sunlight without obscuring the light entirely.

The photograph on the right is a side view from the entrance hall across seemingly endless marble floors into the amazing dining room previously seen on pages 50–1. The antique carved wooden doors frame the view or they can be closed for privacy. When decorating and designing your own home, always remember the important role that doors play. Replacing a run-of-the-mill, store-bought door with an antique one will make all the difference to the overall look of your home, offering originality and uniqueness that everyone will notice and appreciate.

LEFT *A simple French door becomes something quite special when dressed with a lovely antique lace curtain that pools on the floor. The elegant tasseled cord allows an unobstructed view of the backyard beyond.*

RIGHT *With its shiny black and white marble floor and antique wooden doors, this entrance hall exudes grandeur.*

FAR LEFT *This powder room drips gold, from the ornate mirror frame to the hand basin housed in a marble-topped antique console. The look is almost decadent. Gleaming prisms from the sophisticated sconces catch the light.*

LEFT *Soft sophistication is the appeal of this dressing room. Sinuous branches of leaves and flowers trail across the wall mural, creating a suitably feminine backdrop.*

Small rooms need not be insignificant, as shown in the powder room on the far left and the dressing area on this page. The impact of both rooms is enormous simply because they have been decorated correctly.

The first rule of order is not to limit a small room. Many think that bold colors are unsuitable because they make small spaces appear even smaller, but this simply isn't true. A bold color or a mural covering an entire wall can bestow importance so that the size ceases to be noticed. Also, just because a room is small does not mean that it cannot be elegant, filled with important pieces. Antique gold-framed mirrors give both these rooms immediate impact, while the antique console tables enforce the look of timeless elegance.

For me, the exterior of a home is just as important as the interior. This is its drive-by appeal and the first impression everyone has of your home. Take the time to stand out on the street in front of your home and make an evaluation of what can be improved, from the state of the paintwork to the landscaping.

In the photograph below, the amazing array of flowers will put a smile on the face of every passerby. Either side of the stone steps and path, the various plants create a beautiful approach to the house. Ever-blooming rose bushes offer color, together with the flowers of the season. Rosemary, which can be used for cooking, makes for a fabulous drought-tolerant shrub option with a gorgeous scent, while ornamental kale brightens up the garden in the winter.

BELOW *This front yard catches the attention of every passerby and is a wonderful example of inspired landscaping. The stone paths, steps, and wall complement the brickwork of the house perfectly, while the plants have been chosen carefully so that the yard remains pretty throughout the year.*

BELOW RIGHT *Large stone pots of foliage and sumptuous hanging baskets of flowers add color to this backyard oasis. This is the perfect place for a leisurely dip on a hot summer's day.*

Just as when you decorate the inside of your home, in the garden, mix and match by choosing plants of different shapes, types, sizes, height, and vary their numbers. Decide on your colors, then design a planting scheme with plants that flower at different times of the year. Flowers or topiaries can be planted in urns or pots to flank the entrance, where there should be adequate lighting at nighttime for you as you try to get the key in the door and for guests as they await entry.

Peering through the French doors at the rear of the house is the backyard, which does not disappoint. An ivy-covered pool house is where hanging baskets overflow with decadent blooms and foliage, and serve as a backdrop for this fantastic backyard oasis.

*I think of Town and Country
as the best mix of both worlds*

Town and Country

I think of Town and Country style as somewhat modern, always sophisticated, and the best mix of both worlds. I do not believe in too much of any one look in a space or it gets overbearing and boring, so the Town and Country style suits me perfectly. The ultimate Town and Country house should speak of the homeowner's passions, which this home most certainly does. The owner, who has a real love of art and travel, has acquired only the finest pieces over the years and displayed them impeccably.

The entrance hall greets every visitor with a treasure-trove of amazing artwork. Although the pieces might seem to be randomly displayed, everything has in fact been carefully thought through. This kind of display never really happens by chance but takes careful plotting to get just right. Marble busts mingle with gorgeous paintings that cover the walls from top to bottom, while porcelain vases are artworks in themselves. The marble floors and white walls, which give off a definite "town" vibe, serve as a blank canvas, while the only color comes from the objects themselves.

Collecting the pieces for this sort of display takes a lifetime, which is what makes it such an exciting adventure. It amazes me how many people are satisfied by filling their home with wall art, mirrors, and rugs bought from one warehouse store or giant retailer. There is no satisfaction in pieces that you have not hunted and gathered and collected yourself, especially when you acquire them for a drop-dead bargain price out in the middle of a hayfield! That is what it is all about, my friend.

RIGHT *A peek across the stairway and into the entrance hall reveals an amazing collection of artwork that has taken years to acquire. Each piece is displayed to perfection.*

This Town and Country interior is simple yet elegant, pared down to the perfectly picked accessories and creating a modern yet comfortable space. The horns serve as artwork for the walls. The modern shape of the sofa is warmed by the oatmeal color that is also reflected in the drapes.

Modern pieces alone can make for a stark and cold environment, but if they are introduced to a space softened with fabrics and other elements that warm up a room, then the results can be quite superb. Here exotic pink orchid flowers, a favorite of contemporary-style decorators, bring a vibrant splash of color and interest, but their effect is softened by the antique trophy cup in which the plant is displayed.

The study pictured below illustrates exactly what I meant earlier when I said how architectural doors can be used to make a statement in your home. Gothic in style, with an arched surround and decorative wrought ironwork, these dark wooden doors stop everyone in their tracks, and what they have to say is, "I have style and uniqueness." They offer a stunning view into a breathtaking office space. Alcove shelves by the window, filled with favorite books for reference and reading, mimic the curve of the doorway, bringing cohesion to the space. The tiled floor just beyond the door introduces an exotic flavor, while a small chandelier imparts an understated elegance. Like the living space opposite, this study features a delightful mix of favored styles.

LEFT *Simple elegance is the keynote of this living room, where Town and Country merge seamlessly together. Magnificent antlers serve as the artwork on the wall.*

RIGHT *Handsome Gothic-style doors open onto a delightful study, proving that a place of work can be good-looking as well as practical.*

OVERLEAF *The sofa opposite the fireplace gives this living room a contemporary edge, but its oatmeal-colored draperies soften the look so that it fits in perfectly with the other more traditional seating.*

LEFT *Town and Country elements work well together in this entrance hall. A modern glass-topped table displays antique candlesticks and porcelain, flanked by baronial-style cross-base stools.*

RIGHT *Gilt-framed paintings fill the entrance hall and follow the sweeping staircase upward. Their arrangement is meticulous, while the pale painted walls and a neutral floor provide the ideal backdrop.*

An eclectic mix of perfect proportions, this living room has just the right mix of Town and Country. One could sit here for hours just absorbing the surroundings. The space feels modern and sophisticated but contains the right amount of antique artwork to prevent it from being cold and sterile. The owner has collected a really interesting range of antiques of different ages. There are many modern-influenced antiques out there. From art deco to mid-20th century, modern has been a strong influence for decades, and there will always be room in a house for a true modern classic. Having grown up in contemporary

BELOW LEFT *Town meets sophisticated country at the opposite end of the living room featured below right. Neutral flooring and paintwork allow the diverse range of decorative items to look at their best. Turquoise, in the form of glassware and pottery, creates accents of color around the room.*

BELOW *A chandelier shines upon a very chic living room. Artwork, accessories, and stacked books seem almost random in placement, but have actually been placed perfectly to give the eclectic feel.*

surroundings, as a child, I learned early on about the beauty that a Barcelona chair or a reflective mirrored coffee table can possess. The bits of aquamarine blue add a mesmerizing splash of color to a neutral space.

A glance across to the other side of the room reveals even more beautiful pieces of furniture and decorative items, and there is no shortage of unique and interesting lighting either. Everything works together beautifully and reflects the homeowner's personality with an abundance of polish and style.

Decorating a home usually requires a plan. I tend to start with an inspiration of some sort, and that can come from anywhere.

I like the dramatic subtleness of gray, and that was the basis of this dining room's decoration. The walls were painted a charcoal-gray and the rest just really fell into place. A sleek and modern-looking deco chest serves as the buffet, topped with slick gleaming glass and crystal. The wall art above couldn't be simpler: silver serving trays in various sizes, layered with a Venetian mirror and a Venetian frame surrounding an antique black and white print.

A long beveled mirror, running the length of the table, is topped with glass vases, one filled with vintage silver and glass salt and pepper shakers, the other with enormous restaurant serving spoons. Reflecting the candlelight, the mirror makes the table setting sparkle. It just goes to show that you do not have to break the bank to create an interesting collection or tabletop décor.

LEFT *At night, this dining room sparkles. On the table, the beveled mirror from a closet door reflects the light from the chandelier and the twinkling glow of the candles in their mismatching crystal candlesticks. Charcoal-gray walls and tablecloth keep the atmosphere intimate.*

LEFT *Silver and glass are an alluring combination on the buffet. An antique and rare Venetian frame surrounds a one-of-a-kind print. The charcoal-gray paintwork sets the display off perfectly.*

RIGHT *On a beveled mirror from a closet door, glass jars and vases make unusual containers for vintage salt and pepper shakers and silver restaurant serving spoons. The flowers and foliage introduce color and texture to the otherwise monochrome table display. Simple, timeless elegance.*

The sensitive mixing of traditional and industrial elements has created a Town and Country kitchen at its finest

LEFT *Here elements of both town and Country styles sit so well together. A distressed wood island is a vintage flea-market find, while the three lamps add an industrial edge. The dark hardwood floor is a practical and hardwearing surface for this busy, convivial space.*

Impeccable and clean, all in white—with the exception of the distressed wood island—this is a dream Town and Country kitchen if ever I have seen one. The island, discovered at a flea market, turned out to be just the right size and have the perfect patina for the space. It serves as a preparation area and a breakfast bar, forming the focal point of the room. Pretty arrangements of asparagus, cabbage, and leeks on top will soon be tomorrow's dinner but for now they look beautiful as a very unique kind of floral arrangement. Likewise, glass storage jars containing everything from cereal to dog biscuits are decorative additions to the countertops.

Adding to the character of this vintage kitchen re-do, the kitchen cabinets are practical as well as pleasing to the eye, with their glass doors keeping the look light and airy. Like the deep farmhouse sink, the cabinets are traditional in style, but this is offset by the industrial look light fittings suspended over the island and the subway-tile splashbacks.

As always, mixing the old with the new creates the perfect balance

A bedroom needs to be a sanctuary that appeals to all the senses. Unsurprisingly, this bed, a vintage work of art, is the centerpiece of the room. The curlicues and peeling paint give it real presence, and its distressed look is counterbalanced by the absolutely pristine bed linen. A lidded bench at the end of the bed, upholstered in a striking turquoise fabric, is a handsome and practical addition, where you can perch to take off your shoes at the end of a long day. Our signature linen box pillows, used when we want to watch TV on the floor, are piled on top—there is nothing unrelaxing or formal about this room!

Lighting is always important but perhaps more so in the bedroom, where low levels help create a soothing environment. The modern, unfussy pendant light fixture is on a dimmer and in a way sets the tone for the room. Next to the bed, a beautiful vintage cherub lamp base is graced by a more modern shade. As always, mixing the old with the new creates the perfect balance. Simple white linen drapes are truly my absolute favorite. Here, they frame the view of the tree just outside the window beautifully. As I look out, I have the wonderful feeling I am in a tree house.

There are unseen elements in this room that also help to make it a sanctuary. Soft scented powder lightly sprinkled on the sheets serves as aromatherapy while sleeping. The bed linen, which is of the finest quality, is always hung outside to dry—there is nothing quite like the smell of fresh air and sunshine as you settle down to sleep. Everyone should treat themselves to these little inexpensive luxuries.

RIGHT *Many elements work together to turn a bedroom into a sanctuary, where you will feel relaxed and able to unwind. Good-quality bedding and soft lighting soothe the body and soul. The vintage bed, with its curlicue decoration and peeling paint, is gloriously romantic.*

LEFT *With the frame painted a brilliant glossy white, this mirror fits well into a more modern-looking space and stands out as a bold contrast to the brilliant green wall. The classical theme continues in the plaster bust but is counterbalanced by the contemporary-style sofa. An apple-green throw and floral cushions, in the same fabric as the bed linen, break up the expanse of pristine white so the effect is calming, not confrontational.*

RIGHT *Strong accents of green in the fern, martini glass, tray, and botanical prints pull this brave and exciting scheme of lime-green and white together.*

OVERLEAF *The gorgeous bright green is tempered by the white moldings, trim, and accessories in the room. The contrast of the crisp white with the green is great and just what we were looking for to create a space that is contemporary, but anchored with the antique pieces that we love.*

As I mentioned earlier, every house needs refreshing over time, and ours is no exception. This bedroom was admittedly looking rather tired but I only thought about redecorating it when I decided to present my new bedding line from home—there really is nothing quite like an event or a party to prompt one into action!

The green and oatmeal bedding, shown overleaf, was the inspiration behind the room's decoration, and the troops were brought in for a week to complete the work. When I popped the lid on the can of lime-green wall paint, everyone thought that I had lost my mind. I I knew, though, that it would look fresh and modern and not at all overwhelming, as the white moldings, big windows, and white curtains would tone it right down. We brought in some fabulous pieces, both traditional and modern, to create the Town and Country look that I was after. Lime-green accents in both glass, trays, and fabrics, added the desired sparkle. Let me just say that by the time we had finished, this was everyone's favorite room in the house.

Here we have my daughter's bedroom. Like most teenagers, Alex is very picky but when it came to refreshing her room, we did agree that my new Carolyn Westbrook blue and green floral bedding collection, shown overleaf, was perfect with her already aqua walls.

This modern chrome shelf unit gives this corner of the room a focal point, and it is where Alex has chosen to display some of her favorite things. She loves aquariums, fish, and more or less anything to do with the sea. While on a trip to the beach, she bought the gorgeous white shell box, which she displays on top of a couple of very handsome encyclopedias. A white ironstone pedestal, meanwhile, makes the perfect container for her collection of white shells.

Every teenager loves magazines, and this white and chrome director's chair and ottoman by the window make a great spot to flip through fashion magazines. Dressing the windows are my most favored white linen curtains, which are accented beautifully by glossy black curtain rods.

In the photograph overleaf, you can see much more of the room. Alex does like contemporary design, so we brought in other modern elements to make it "her" style, such as the abstract painting of ballerinas over the bed and the mirrored tray for holding favorite keepsakes and jewelry boxes.

OPPOSITE *Suitably modern to suit Alex's style, the chrome shelving unit shows off her favorite memorabilia beautifully. The petite lamp introduces a classical element.*

LEFT *Leather-bound encyclopedias form the base for displaying Alex's treasured box of shells. The neutral colors of the books and shells complement each other well and look striking against the contrasting aqua wall.*

OVERLEAF *When it came to refreshing this bedroom, the aqua-painted walls remained because they suited my new floral bedding collection so well. The bedding and drapes are quite traditional in appeal, as are the French-style mirror and dresser. As a counterbalance, accents of black in the layering of shag rugs, curtain rods, and tray give a modern edge.*

We should always surround ourselves with the things we love

Alex has learned well from my belief that we should always surround ourselves with the things we love. One of her particular interests is photography and she loves to take pictures. She has some really interesting ones, and rather than have them hidden away in a box, we decided to make a wall collection of her favorites featuring her with her friends, some from a school photography project, others just random shots. It was not an expensive proposition. We housed the photographs in clear plastic box frames, which adds to the contemporary appeal of the room. Now she can enjoy them every day as they hang above the sofa. This pretty piece of furniture was moved into the room from elsewhere to serve as seating whenever her friends come to visit. Obviously teenagers need a spot to hang out and watch movies, so it was important to create a room that would not only be beautiful but also functional.

Alex had a passion for all that was French long before she ever visited the country, and this is reflected in her room's décor, from the artwork to the ornate mirror and French-style dresser. Her favorite Paris print of the Eiffel Tower commands attention where it hangs over the fireplace mantel. The frame provides further accents of black in the room, along with an old concrete fruit basket and some tiny cherubs that support a stack of miniature-size classic books. *Très magnifique.*

LEFT *Modern plastic box frames suit the subject matter of these photographs perfectly. Symmetrically placed, they create an eyecatching display.*

RIGHT *Black accents from the Parisian print and ornaments on the mantel add to those already in the room, highlighting its contemporary edge.*

I love the sense of drama created by combining black and white

Black and White

LEFT *An arrangement of antique roses in every shade of pink gives an amazing blast of color to an otherwise monochrome table setting.*

OVERLEAF *A color scheme of black and white gives the kitchen a modern and sophisticated feel, which is softened by the decorative metal chandelier and the pedestal container filled with antique roses.*

I love the sense of drama that the combination of black and white creates, and I have used it throughout my house. When we first embarked on the kitchen renovation, we opted for black cabinets, which were unheard of at the time. I thought they set off the white countertops and sink perfectly.

The decorative details of the kitchen change constantly. I have various collections of antique dishes, and I like to use them all, so I swap them around so that each collection can be appreciated at some time or other. In this photograph, the table is set with the dishes that I grew up with—simple yet elegant white plates in an octagon shape that look striking against the black tablecloth. Here it is all about the flowers—absolutely fabulous antique roses in every hue, from hot pink to pale pink, that are bursting forth from a wonderful white Italian pedestal container. Black and white monogram napkins add the finishing detail.

RIGHT *The black and white drama continues in the sun porch. White-painted paneled walls and a white floor supply the blank canvas for the accents of black. There is something "Out of Africa" to the room, with the zebra rug, binoculars, and floor-to-ceiling striped curtains reminiscent of a Bedouin tent.*

The sun porch had what you might call an extreme re-do, being transformed from reds and blues to black and white. Once we had decided that this would be the room's new look, we hunted down all the wonderful black and white treasures that we already had and also added a few new ones. This is the fun part—finding the perfect collectibles to create the perfect atmosphere.

LEFT *Bold, vertical striped curtains, with their oversized horizontal-striped hem, set the tone for this dramatic sun porch. Uncompromising modern elements in the room such as these are tempered by the vintage dove cage and classic-style lamp with its frilly edged shade, given extra height by the antique books. The mirror-topped bamboo side table is a useful addition to the room alongside the love seat, but it is also a display surface. Crucial to the success of any room's decoration is a living element, provided here by the potted palm.*

The vintage dove cage makes a pretty decorative feature by the window where it is framed by the bold floor-to-ceiling curtains. The zebra rug, another bold element, is one of my favorite pieces. Used here, it seems to bring all the disparate elements of the room together. Anyone who knows me knows that I love the whole "Out of Africa" look, and this room is a little reminiscent of that.

RIGHT *A photograph taken of the base of the Eiffel Tower in Paris becomes a piece of art when held fast between the needles of an old flower frog. The milk-glass compote is filled with vintage wooden croquet balls.*

Redecorating a space gives one the best excuse
to go shopping for collectibles

BELOW *A dramatic display is created with some out-of-the-box thinking. Layers of gesso give the vintage deer head an unconventional look, exaggerated even more by the glossy black frame set at an angle surrounding it. A vintage zebra rug brings together the look of black and white fabulously.*

BELOW *Peering at my daughter's charcoal drawing is the dog that forms part of the sentimental pen and ink holder that once belonged to my grandfather. Items of emotional significance such as these make a display even more powerful. A splash of green from the potted fern unites the various elements.*

Another view of the sun porch reveals some pretty creative decorating. I revamped a vintage deer's head by slicking down all of it with gesso. Once I had covered it several times, I then painted it with glossy white paint. It is now the centerpiece of the wall, poking through an antique glossy black-painted frame and surmounted by some interesting black and white horn mounts. Charcoal drawings by my daughter Victoria, which hadn't really found a home up until now, fit in beautifully on the table below.

Redecorating a space gives you the best excuse to go shopping for collectibles that will complement what you already have to create the most incredible space. I knew that the black-beaded chandelier would fit in perfectly here, shining down on the concrete garden cherub atop a glossy white French table. Alongside, a re-created London subway sign makes for a great conversation piece.

LEFT *Flanking the French chest are two French glossy black chairs with cane backs, cushioned with white linen and ruffles. A re-created London subway sign introduces an idiosyncratic note.*

A long hallway creates plenty of drama with the seemingly endless stretch of shiny black and white checkerboard marble floor extending into the kitchen. The view is very inviting—a collection of cast-iron skillets, graduated in size, hang over the stove for easy access but also for decoration, alongside a vase of hydrangeas, proving that a kitchen does not have to be purely utilitarian.

Storage and organization are the key to any cook's success, and by using vintage elements and containers, one can be organized, functional, and stylish. Introducing vintage elements will give the space character. Here, a wooden cabinet, its chipped paint adding to its charm, offers storage for a collection of cookbooks in the bottom cupboard, while the open shelves are used for storing other kitchen essentials.

LEFT *The hallway appears almost infinite as it flows dramatically into the kitchen along a sea of black and white checkerboard floor tiles. The wallpaper continues the color scheme but, unlike the floors, its design is far from geometric, which softens the space.*

RIGHT *This vintage wooden cupboard with accents of black, white, and green makes charming and practical storage for a range of kitchen necessities, including favorite cookbooks and traditional flour and bread bins. A vintage green "cake" tin is filled with rolls of twine, tape, kitchen shears, and all those small bits and pieces that are hard to find a home for. An ironstone pot serves as a planter.*

OVERLEAF *This garden patio is the ultimate in sophisticated outdoor relaxation, with a handsome black and white striped parasol complemented by the seat cushions on curlicue metal chairs. Vivid green ferns and palms and brick paving soften the space and ensure a warm welcome.*

Being bold in your decorative choices is essential for a small space

LEFT *Gorgeous French-inspired toile de Jouy wallpaper forms the dramatic background to this small bathroom, which has been turned into an incredible space by the bold decorating choices. Bringing a touch of glamour is the gilt carved mirror, a work of art in itself, which doubles the impact of the wallpaper. This is complemented by the classical-style column and acts as a pedestal for the classical lamp base, setting it at just the right height.*

With a small bathroom, there is all the more reason to turn it into an incredible space, and there are many tricks that will help you to achieve just that. Any bathroom can be made beautiful with paint or wallpaper but being bold in your decorative choices is essential for one that is small. Difficult to ignore here is the toile de Jouy wallpaper in a very dramatic black and cream, and its impact is doubled, reflected in the carved mirror and the sconces. Turning your back on convention with your choice of shower curtain is another way to make the room special. A curtain that you make yourself from a fabulous fabric will easily surpass a generic store-bought one, which are often too short and skimpy anyway. You can also take the fabric all the way to the ceiling, which will make the bathroom appear that much larger.

Accents of black on the vanity introduce an element of sophistication. Small black stones offset the white soap in the soap dish, and a pink and black French transferware platform is used to hold jewelry. The towels, meanwhile, combine black and white, the ultimate in sophisticated style.

Another small bathroom tucked just above the staircase is painted a solid black to serve as a backdrop for a beautiful, sparkling Venetian mirror. This is one of my favorite pieces, which I brought back from Paris, and the black paint allows it to be appreciated in all its glory. To the side are vintage bookplates featuring shells, framed in modern mirrored frames, adding to the sparkle of the wall.

Here, the vanity, which is none too special, has been given a toile skirt, to provide useful as well as attractive concealed storage. You can also decant various bathroom essentials into decorative containers, to bring an unexpected element of beauty. In this bathroom, mouthwash, originally in a plastic container, has been stored in an etched glass bottle. A huge old store jar, brought back from France, is filled with fragrant bars of soap. A pink rose, to match the hand towel, and a white hydrangea have been brought in from the garden, creating a fresh look. Fresh and fluffy white towels, meanwhile, are stacked on a shelf. Pretty and functional… what could be better?

LEFT A plain black wall allows the gorgeous Venetian mirror, the centerpiece of this bathroom, to be appreciated without distraction.

BELOW left A glossy modern-style lamp sets off a small Venetian mirror, which reflects a lovely etched bottle of mouthwash.

BELOW Even a functional bathroom should be made to look attractive. Fresh blooms, brought in for color and beauty, are presented in vintage glassware. An otherwise unassuming silver serving platter acts as an upmarket soap dish.

The Making of a Collection

You might think of a collection as just a bunch of knickknacks of no particular significance, but that is not the case. A collection has to have special meaning for you, otherwise it will feel out of place in your home. That said, it can comprise virtually any gathering of favorite things. As you have probably realized, I am an avid collector—our home is full of collections—and that means I collect anything that strikes my fancy. Over the years, this has ranged from garden cherubs to antique bookplates of botanical paintings. Who knows what it will be next?

Our collections are as individual as our personalities, reflecting our interests and passions. They can be inspired by a color combination, a certain style of art, or simply by the love of a particular object. Forming a collection gives a person a reason to go out shopping or hunting for the prize, which is, of course, whatever it is you are collecting at the time. Happy hunting!

RIGHT *A large wall can be a daunting space to fill. Like an extension of the buffet, this well-ordered and symmetrical display of framed antique bookplates makes a beautiful collection on the wall.*

BELOW *Nestled in among the greenery, stone cherubs representing the four seasons make an unusual but inspired garden collection.*

BELOW RIGHT *A mesmerizing mix of different shades of blue and white creates a warm welcome at the entry porch here at the plantation. Mismatching patterns and fabrics give the setting an altogether more informal feel.*

BELOW *On the opposite side of the porch, a rebellious element in the form of a red and blue plaid seat cushion is introduced to the blue mix. The red is picked out in the petunais on the glass-topped table, unifying the scheme.*

Blue and white makes for such a striking display and here it is shown off beautifully on the front porch at the plantation. I took my time finding just the right pots, vases, and jars that would blend together perfectly. The same can be said for the fabric in the custom-made cushions and pillows. There are many fabrics of different textures and shades of blue gathered here, which make for an altogether more interesting collage of hues than could be achieved with just one fabric. We often continue to use this space during fall and winter when the weather can still be quite warm at the plantation. A plaid throw in just the right colors is tossed across the arm of a wicker sofa for those cooler nights.

LEFT When creating a collection for display, such as these natural history prints, it is important that there is a cohesion of color, not only in the objects themselves but also in the background. The Chinese porcelain vase and two plates in the niche give added interest.

RIGHT An impressive collection of brown transferware took time and real dedication to acquire. Every shape and size of plate is here, masterfully displayed on a large paneled wall. The brown of the sconces and framed antique map suit the scheme perfectly.

I just would like to say that not only is silver beautiful and comes in all kinds of pieces, from silverware to serving pieces to antique serving domes, but it should be a necessity to anyone starting out or who entertains…ever. There is nothing quite like a bundle of antique hotel silverware or really any antique silverware. It does not have to be sterling and the silverplate version can be found very inexpensively at estate sales and garage sales. Anyone who eats from a fork deserves a good utensil and not the lightweight, flimsy, almost disposable versions that are sold in stores today. If you just take the time to find it, the good stuff is out there my friend, waiting to be collected by you.

BELOW LEFT *All shapes and sizes of antique hotel serving domes, as beautiful as they are functional, are displayed in my kitchen.*

RIGHT *Napkin rings are for me a much more convenient alternative to a perfectly folded napkin. Antique silver rings with linen napkins add an element of sophistication to any meal. Like silverware, they are often monogrammed.*

BELOW RIGHT *An unlikely collection of intricately cut vintage glass salt and pepper shakers adds a bit of sparkle to the table.*

BELOW *As well as making a table setting that much more special, antique silverware from flea markets and secondhand stores are often much cheaper than their poor-quality, mass-retail counterparts.*

A carefully thought-out collection of artwork

is essential to any home

RIGHT *A carefully thought-out collection of artwork is essential to any home, adding interest, color, and beauty to an otherwise blank canvas. Here, perfectly matched frames with not an inch of space between them create the impression of one single piece of art. The gold frames were deliberately chosen to complement the faucets and mirror.*

BELOW *Displayed in a silver tray on the desk is one of my favorite collectibles ever—tartanware. These highly sought-after boxes come in various plaids and an assortment of colors, and are very rare and hard to find. In this sophisticated and masterfully planned interior, they look right at home.*

LEFT *A marvelous and unique collection of the woman's form perfectly shown off in alabaster. As you can see, the woman is again reflected in the drapery fixture.*

RIGHT *Here again, an elegant and interesting collection of many different beautiful alabaster and porcelain components.*

In this big city house, we witness the art of collecting at its finest. Such a grand collection did not just happen—it took time to amass all the right components of religious art and etchings, and has been very carefully planned. The assortment of frames and sizes adds to the interest of the display, as does the lack of color, which I think looks marvelous with the room's surroundings. The artwork itself is amazing, with each piece telling a story. It is hard to say what the focal point of the room is, with the curvaceous mantel competing with the wall display. It can only be decided by the eye of the beholder but, I am sure you will agree, they are both works of art.

LEFT *The religious wall art in this sitting room has been carefully chosen and expertly put together for a breathtaking result. One could stand for hours admiring and interpreting each piece, and that is the real beauty of collecting.*

chapter two

Farmhouse Living

• Farmhouse Life • The Grounds
• A Fisherman's Cabin

Farmhouse Life

What could be better than farmhouse living? This is exactly what I dreamed of twenty years ago, when we made the move from the city. I dreamed of chickens and gardens and space, and not looking out the window directly into someone else's home.

It all came as a huge culture shock for us at first. The enormous, rambling plantation, sprawled out on 53 acres, was in need of much work… but now I would not trade it for the world. It gets dark here at night, I mean really dark. There are no city lights for miles but, instead, the stars shine like diamonds. We can throw a rock and not hit our neighbor's house, and the green grass seems to go on forever and begs us to lie down and gaze up at the clear, blue sky.

The chickens have a happy life here, too, accommodated in the chicken coop that is original to the plantation. We have spruced it up a bit over the years, given it a coat of whitewash and added an outdoor patio, but it is still essentially the same.

LEFT *Chik-Fil-a, seen here strutting his stuff, is the only man allowed in the hen house. Rather than run around outside, this rooster decided life was better spent inside the cage, if he wanted to stay alive.*

RIGHT *Our chickens live a grand farmhouse life in their rustic coop, which is original to the plantation. They have plenty of time to go about their daily business of clucking, scratching, and laying eggs, which we collect every morning for breakfast. The eggs come in all colors, shapes, and sizes, and are as varied as our chickens.*

This is a way of life that I would not trade for anything

Living the farmhouse life is certainly very different from life in the city. It allows you to slow down the pace and discover different interests. To appreciate the beauty of nature, all you have to do is look out the window. Horses in the field trot over when they see us approaching. They nudge at us, wanting a pet on the nose or a back rub and, of course, to be fed some delectable hay. I wanted our children to be able to grow up with nature and animals, and lead a life that had a care-free quality about it, something the city could never offer. I was not a complete city slicker when we arrived here, having spent summers on my grandparents' farm, but I had no idea about certain aspects of country life, like poison ivy or chicken snakes. We have learned all these things over the years, and my kids can be found fishing or relaxing in the three-story tree house that they built overlooking the pond across the road.

It is funny to me how farmhouse life has become a hot commodity and people everywhere are getting in on the action for reality shows and such. This is just how it is here, the real farmhouse life, as you see it, and a real everyday pleasure for us as we are able to till the ground, to make a garden that will provide a bounty to be used all year long. It is a way of life that I would not trade for anything and a place that feels like home.

ABOVE *Horses wait patiently in line for their daily feed of hay from a vintage truck.*

ABOVE LEFT *Gypsy outsmarts the other horses and helps herself.*

OPPOSITE, ABOVE LEFT *Even the chicken coop is lit by candlelight! After all, everyone needs a delightful atmosphere, especially our ladies that rule the roost.*

OPPOSITE, ABOVE RIGHT *We have several wheelbarrows but this is our favorite. It's very old and rusty, but never gets a flat.*

OPPOSITE, BELOW LEFT *Araucana eggs in pale blues and greens are always a favorite of the clutch and make for great decorating opportunities.*

OPPOSITE, BELOW RIGHT *With their fluffy hair-dos, Minnie and Pearl, the Polish hens, stand out among the ladies of the house.*

The Grounds

Here at The Plantation a potting shed is a necessity and this porch is loaded with style and function. The building is a lesson in history and was known as the doctor's office long ago. It was in great disrepair when we moved here—the porch had to be rebuilt and shutters were added to the front. Antique organza curtains peek from inside, and pots of all shapes and sizes line the front. The grounds surrounding the house cover two acres, with lots of gardens that have to be tended. Trails of brick-lined walks surrounded by beds of groundcover, shrubberies, and lots of flowers are everywhere, not to mention the herb and vegetable gardens. This is where plants are repotted and seedlings are carefully coddled. Here this old zinc-top table proves to be the perfect place for work, where dirt and water are mixed to create something beautiful.

BELOW LEFT *The bee skep, perched on a classical column, was discovered at a flea market. Both pieces contribute hugely to the charm of the porch.*

BELOW *Glass cloches protect young seedlings from the late winter frost. A metal bird, rusty with age, makes a lovely decorative addition to the table.*

RIGHT *A child's wheelbarrow has found its rightful home on the porch, as there is always a child around to learn the importance and fun of gardening.*

OVERLEAF *Once known as the doctor's office, the potting shed has a rustic charm all of its own, with decorative pieces interspersed among terra-cotta pots and glass cloches. When the good life gets too much, there is a weather-beaten seat, piled high with cushions, for taking a snooze.*

LEFT *An assortment of cloches are on hand for covering seedlings or sometimes simply as decoration. The architectural piece, propped up against the wall, is used as a shelf.*

RIGHT *We are always salvaging broken pieces of concrete, and this statue of a cherub had ended up on the ground surrounded by clover. It made for an irresistible photo.*

A Fisherman's Cabin

Our fisherman's cabin is original to the plantation. Surrounded by woods and wildlife, it stands close to our two-acre pond in a thicket of trees. It is very rustic in nature, and in its decoration I have enjoyed mixing the decadent with the decaying.

A porch serves as a spot to hang your hat from the antler hooks, drop your fishing poles, and take off your boots. As you step inside, you are seduced by the cabin's primitive charm. Gaps between the logs allow in chinks of light. The widest gaps are covered with mosquito netting, partly for practical reasons but also because I love the hazy illusion it creates. The cabin is masculine in its decoration but also comfortable, with a time-worn leather club chair and a bed casually dressed in oatmeal linen. This is where my son and his friends can meet up, and where the men can relax and have a drink after a day of fishing or hunting.

LEFT *An old army cot, covered in a ticking stripe vintage mattress, is the perfect tranquil spot for taking a nap in the midst of the thicket of trees. Horn mounts that came with the cabin are used as hanging racks for various pieces of fishing and hunting paraphernalia.*

RIGHT *Crumpled newspaper on the table contains the latest catch about to be enjoyed with crusty French bread and a nip of something warming!*

OVERLEAF *Inside the cabin, it's possible to rough it with many of the comforts of home, from the leather club chair to a bed dressed in white and brown linen.*

LEFT *A tiny vintage collection of moths is displayed in a delightfully rustic wooden frame, which appears to blend with the wood of the walls.*

RIGHT *A vintage travel trunk provides storage and a display surface for a few of my favorite things—wicker bottles, trophy cups, and leather-bound antique books. Hanging from the wall above, and appropriate decoration for a fisherman's cabin, are a grand old fish platter and a fabulous old print of sea fare.*

chapter three

Gatherings and Celebrations

• A Spring Gathering • An Autumn Harvest Table

• A Plantation Christmas

A Spring Gathering

It is always a good time for a party is what I say, and I use any excuse to throw one. I love to get together with friends and family, and such an event always motivates me to get on with any outstanding cleaning and decorating. As soon as the birds start to chirp in the mornings and I see the first robin hopping about on the green grass, it makes me want to be outdoors. A spring gathering is a wonderful idea for the family, and eating outdoors is always a treat.

Although this set-up looks elaborate, you could do the same in your own backyard. Vintage porch posts are sandwiched between two harvest tables, while metal rails run over the top of the tables, covered in wisteria vines. Simple wooden benches and metal garden chairs provide the seating. This tabletop is all about the garden and the color pink. A peeling pink cherub surrounded by greenery with pink accents and a potted pink hydrangea make appropriate centerpieces.

RIGHT *Accents of pink make this party table very pretty indeed. Even the potted plant has pink running through its veins. Presiding over it all is a peeling pink cherub.*

BELOW LEFT *A pink hydrangea, surrounded by a compote and strawberry-filled pastries, is the centerpiece on the second table.*

BELOW *Exotic-looking jars make the candy appear all the more tempting.*

OVERLEAF *Wisteria vines offer shade over these harvest tables laden with delights. Hanging from a branch is a crystal chandelier that tinkles like a bell in the breeze.*

An Autumn Harvest Table

A change in season always seems a good time to celebrate and get together with friends and family. We are fortunate to live in a warmer climate in Texas but sometimes, in the summer, the heat can become so tiring that when the first cool breezes blow, it always makes for a bit of excitement in the air. And that's my excuse to eat outside in candlelight.

Candlelight always makes for a dreamy environment. Here, an old chandelier hanging from the tree glows invitingly, while the table is dotted with candles. Pumpkins are in abundance and are harvested from the gardens. Carved and with a tea light inside, they make wonderful luminaries lining the porch steps, as well as decoration for the table. This setting couldn't be simpler—an ordinary table has been covered with a white drop cloth, then topped with a piece of contrasting burlap (hessian). Buffet style makes it easy to prepare for a party and creates a more relaxed atmosphere. Plates are stacked and utensils are held in spooners and ironstone for easy access. I still love to have a little formality outdoors—I cherish the whole unexpectedness of it. That's why I chose to use my favorite brown transferware and real silverware, not paper plates or plastic knives and forks. You only live once, so what's the point in hiding the good stuff away? Use it to make your party more memorable. Your guests will definitely appreciate the gesture.

LEFT *It is the unexpected touches that make a festive gathering special. Hanging from the tree is a metal chandelier that glows with magical candlelight just above the table. China plates, real silverware, and crystal goblets make guests feel honored. In spite of this, the atmosphere is informal, with a linen dropcloth and a piece of burlap covering the table and simple wooden benches providing the seating.*

RIGHT *Pumpkins are harvested to add color to the table, while crystal goblets wait to be filled with iced tea. Twinkling candles in glass jars bring romance.*

A Plantation Christmas

I love the Christmas holidays—it is absolutely my favorite time of year. The excitement is such that the Thanksgiving meal is barely finished and we are already grabbing the trimmings from the attic. There are boxes and boxes of sparkle, glitter, ornaments, and greenery that must all take their place to make this holiday decorating season better than the last. A garland of greenery, ribbons, and lights is draped along the entire white plank fence in front of the plantation, while fresh, green Christmas wreaths adorn the columns flanking the drive, welcoming all who visit here. The entrance doors, too, are dressed with wreaths, as well as garlands and a central decoration filled with fruit, greenery, and red plaid bows. Hanging from the balcony over the entrance is a giant wreath with ribbons and bows. But let us not forget the twinkle lights! Thousands and thousands of them are woven about the house to cast an unforgettable, magical glow that can only be called "Christmas."

BELOW *Starting with the white plank fence, the plantation is bedecked in her holiday finest to pay tribute to the season.*

RIGHT *Live greenery of wreaths and garlands surrounds the doorway, extending a warm welcome to all who enter for the holiday season.*

There is no place like home for the holidays

Once inside, the plantation house seems to explode with the sights and smells of the season. The Christmas tree and greenery give off the evergreen scent that reminds you of childhood wishes and sugarplum dreams. A garland of greenery, bows, ribbons, ornaments, and hundreds of sparkling lights cascades down the stair railing. I am always covered in glitter and sparkle when the decorating is done but then I can sit back and enjoy being with my family at this special time of year. We keep up the traditions here, and the teenagers are always eager to try out cookie baking and canning. Friends and family look forward to their homemade jalapeño jelly that has become a tradition here since my son Nicholas started harvesting jalapeños from the garden.

There really is no place like home for the holidays. Every part of the house is decorated and that includes the kitchen. The Welsh dresser is piled high with greenery, red transferware, and plaid plates. An old marshmallow tin holds jars of different heights, which are filled with candy canes and freshly baked sugar cookies, to form the centerpiece of the kitchen table. The decorations and adornments seem to flow through the house, much like the laughter and sweet smells that Christmas is all about.

FAR LEFT *The greenery is plentiful and gives off the heavenly scent of the holidays as it cascades down the stair railing. Hundreds of twinkle lights, entwined through the garland, add to the festive charm.*

TOP LEFT *Gilded feathers, velvety embossed ribbons, and glistening pine cones and branches are brought together to form a breathtaking look.*

LEFT *The fresh green garland is laced with icy branches and adorned with brown velvet and green silk ribbons for a glorious look.*

RIGHT *Even my treasured antique German animals join in the Christmas celebrations, laced with vintage beads. Bursting out of antique trophy cups are vintage silver bead sprays, resembling flowers in a vase.*

155

LEFT *The living room always houses the family Christmas tree, which is covered with decorations that go back over the generations. Many are homemade, from popsicle (ice lolly) sticks and pill jars covered in glitter. They are all very special to us as a family, with each one holding a cherished memory.*

BELOW *The mantel is filled with greenery, berries, pine cones, and ribbons in the traditional colors of Christmas. The red walls and jaunty jockey in his red breeches, which are present year-round, seem tailor-made for the festivities.*

Index

Acknowledgments

It takes a village, as they say, especially when putting together a book. I am grateful to all of those who gave me the honor of being a part of my book, and it is all the better for it.

I wanted to dedicate this book to Jack (the big black lab) who always met me at the end of the road (2003–2011) who I miss every time that I turn the corner, and to my favorite dog in the whole world—Princess, my black schnauzer, who was a bit sassy, and loved and protected the entire family (2002–2011). You both will be missed.

To David Peters and Cindy Richards, whom I adore and respect—thanks for believing in me. You two are great people to work with and great fun whether over dinner or in the middle of a hayfield in Texas. Love to you both. To my editor Gillian Haslam, I could not ask for anyone better. You are amazing at your job and a real pleasure to work with. To Kevin Haas, who has to sell these books for Pete's sake. He even met me at a book signing with all women, and ended up having a great time, sipping a "craftini."

I would like to thank my fantastic photography team, who are now like part of the family. They like coming to Texas, as much as I like going to New York. Here's to Keith and Eric… Next time may you not eat so many jalapeños you make yourselves sick!

Thanks to Phil and Cathy for believing in me and for introducing me to a wonderful and creative person… Jan. Thanks to Jan and Bob Barstad, for opening up their beautiful home. It was a great pleasure to meet Jan, who always has a smile on her face, and obviously has great taste.

Thanks to the wonderful gathering of friends, who all have fantastic homes and a fantastic sisterhood. They are all a joy, including Joy Hudson and her friends who took part: Chris Coates and Sue Jones. Thanks to my friends Gwen and Bill Baum, who have a fantastic home right outside of New York City… and to Bill's masterful collection and placement of beautiful artwork. These are two people who are as nice as they are talented and I am honored to call them my friends.

Since most of the book was shot here at The Plantation, I have to thank my family, who has an undying dedication to helping me with projects, no matter how crazy.

To Joe, the lifelong partner who is always there for me, even when it includes painting a house pink or ripping up tack strip in the middle of the night.

To my mother Charlotte, who is the most unbelievable taste maker, trendsetter, and still on top of everything, as the queen of decorating. I owe all that I am to you.

To my Dad, who always has the solution to any problem. Love you.

To my son Nick, who is an incredible young man. He takes care of whatever I ask him to, whether it is putting up holiday lights, mowing the field, or giving me his design advice. You are incredible, and I love you dearly.

To Victoria, who is an incredible young lady and an activist for the greater good. I honestly do not know how she does all the things that she does in a day and still manages to have a 4.0 in school. When she is not studying, she is trying to make the world a better place, and she has more courage than I ever will. Standing up for those in need, even when it is tough, and always a friend to the friendless. I love you and hope that all of your dreams come true.

To Alexandria, my fashionista and my academic. She has grown up in a world of fashion and design and now loves clothing fashion herself. She is independent and beautiful and smart… a triple threat. All my love to you.

To Christian, who came down for a summer break and ended up working on a photo shoot in 110 degree weather, and who tells me that no matter how much I make, it is not worth it. Love you and thanks for all of your help!

To Christi, thanks for being there for me when I needed it. Much love to you. Cannot leave out Carrington, who is too little to really help, but who pointed at one of the pictures in my last book, and asked where that place was, that it was beautiful and she wanted to have a room just like it. She is my little protegé.

Thanks to my friends and manufacturer in New York who partnered with me to create the Carolyn Westbrook Home bedding line that is featured in and on the cover of this book. We are working hard to make the Carolyn Westbrook Home bedding available at a retailer in your neighborhood. Thanks, and here's to Steve, Ellen, Harry, Dewey, Randy, Heath, Catalina, and Sonya.

To Bob, who is always looking out for my best interest..

To Tim, thanks for believing in me and joining the team.

Most importantly, thanks to every single one of you that bought this book. When I am doing a book, I always try and make every page meaningful and hopefully along the way give someone the inspiration that they need to create a lovely home. I hope that you enjoy.

xo Carolyn

www.carolynwestbrookhome.com

Common Core
Standards Practice Workbook

Teacher Guide

Grade 3

Glenview, Illinois • Boston, Massachusetts
Chandler, Arizona • Upper Saddle River, New Jersey

ISBN-13: 978-0-328-75693-3
ISBN-10:   0-328-75693-8

3 4 5 6 7 8 9 10 V069 19 18 17 16 15 14 13

Grade 3 Contents

Standards Practice

Assessment

Teacher Support

About this Guide

Pearson is pleased to offer this **Common Core Standards Practice** Teacher's Guide, a companion to the **Common Core Standards Practice Workbook.** It includes these pages:

- **Common Core Standards Practice pages.** Two pages of practice exercises for each Common Core State Standard. Students will find different kinds of exercises that are similar to the items expected to be on the Next Generation Assessment that students will be taking starting in 2014–2015.

- **Practice for the Common Core Assessment.** Each Practice Assessment consists of one (1) Practice End-of-Year Assessment and two (2) Performance Tasks. One Practice Assessment is found in the Student Workbook, while the second is a "secure" test found only in this Teacher's Guide. The two Practice End-of-Year Assessments are mirror assessments.

  The Practice End-of-Year assessment was built to align to the content emphases of both PARCC and SBAC. That means that 70% of the items assess major content emphases. In addition, many of the items are similar to the innovative items that are expected to be on the upcoming Next Generation Assessments. Students will encounter multiple-response selected-response items; simulated technology-enabled items that ask students to sort answer options into appropriate categories or to construct responses on grids, graphs, and number lines; constructed response items that ask them to explain their reasoning or justify their thinking; and extended constructed response items that include multi-part questions with multi-step solutions. The Performance Tasks present students with problem situations in real-world context and ask students to make use of their developing proficiency with the Standards for Mathematical Practice and their firmer understanding of Math Content to find solutions.

- Answers to all of the student pages as 4-ups.

- **Correlation Chart for the Practice EOY Assessment.** The chart indicates for each item the Content Standard assessed and lessons in *enVisionMATH™ Common Core* and sessions in *Investigations in Number, Data, and Space® for the Common Core* where students can go for more practice of the standard assessed.

- **Scoring Rubrics for the four (4) Performance Tasks.** In additional to recommendations for scoring, these pages list both the Standards for Mathematical Practice and Mathematical Content that the task assesses.

Common Core Standards Practice and Assessments

Name _____

Common Core Standards Practice

3.OA.A.1 Interpret products of whole numbers, e.g., interpret 5 × 7 as the total number of objects in 5 groups of 7 objects each.

1. Molly has 3 packs of pencils. Each pack holds 8 pencils. Molly writes 3 × 8 to represent the problem situation. What does 3 × 8 show?

2. There are 5 kittens. Each kitten has 4 legs. What expression can represent the total number of legs?

3. Write a problem story that matches 7 × 3.

4. Explain why your story matches 7 × 3.

 3

5. Write a word problem story that matches 3×5.

6. Explain why your story matches 3×5.

7. Brad planted 6 rows of flowers. He planted 4 flowers in each row. Tell why 6×4 gives the total number of flowers Brad planted.

8. Marco buys 4 bags of apples. There are 10 apples in each bag. Tell why 4×10 gives the total number of apples.

Name _____

Common Core Standards Practice

3.OA.A.2 Interpret whole-number quotients of whole numbers, e.g., interpret 56 ÷ 8 as the number of objects in each share when 56 objects are partitioned equally into 8 shares, or as a number of shares when 56 objects are partitioned into equal shares of 8 objects each.

1. Sally is putting 32 muffins on 8 plates. Each plate has the same number of muffins. What expression shows how many muffins are on each plate?

2. Jon has 24 oranges. He puts 6 oranges in each bag. What expression shows how many bags John needs?

3. Write a problem story that matches 42 ÷ 7.

4. Explain why your problem matches 42 ÷ 7.

5. Write a problem story that matches 27 ÷ 3.

6. Explain why your problem story matches 27 ÷ 3.

7. There are 56 students sitting at 8 tables. Each table has the same number of students. What expression can tell the number of students at each table.

8. Ruben wants to buy 18 tennis balls. There are 3 balls in each can. What expression can tell the number of cans Ruben will need to buy?

Name _____

Common Core Standards Practice

3.OA.A.3 Use multiplication and division within 100 to solve word problems in situations involving equal groups, arrays, and measurement quantities, e.g., by using drawings and equations with a symbol for the unknown number to represent the problem.

1. Hannah has 3 bags of marbles. In each bag are 6 marbles.

   a. Draw a picture to match to problem.

   b. How many marbles does Hannah have? _____

2. There are 16 stamps arranged into 4 equal rows.

   a. Draw an array to match the problem.

   b. How many stamps are in each row? _____

3. Five friends are at the school fair. They have 25 ride tickets that they will share evenly. Each friend gets the same number. For 3a–3d, choose Yes or No to indicate whether each number sentence could be used to find the number of tickets each friend gets.

   a. $25 \times 5 = \square$ YES   NO

   b. $25 \div 5 = \square$ YES   NO

   c. $5 \times \square = 25$ YES   NO

   d. $5 \div \square = 25$ YES   NO

4. Ms Donovan sets up her classroom with 4 rows of desks.
Each row has 5 desks.

    a. Draw an array to show how many desks Mrs. Donovan has in her classroom.

    b. How many desks are there in all? _____

5. Sherri has 24 inches of yarn. She cuts the yarn into pieces that are each 6 inches long.

    a. Write an equation to show how many pieces of yarn Sherri has.

    _____

    b. How many pieces of yarn does Sherri have? _____

6. Roger's father has 6 pieces of wood. Each piece is 8 inches long. For 6a–6d, choose Yes or No to indicate whether each number sentence could be used to find how many inches of wood Roger's father has.

    a. $8 \times 6 = \Box$ YES   NO

    b. $8 \div 6 = \Box$ YES   NO

    c. $\Box \times 6 = 8$ YES   NO

    d. $\Box \div 6 = 8$ YES   NO

Name _____

Common Core Standards Practice

3.OA.A.4 Determine the unknown whole number in a multiplication or division equation relating three whole numbers.

1. Write a multiplication number sentence to match this story problem.

   Maddy needs to fill 6 baskets with canned goods for the food drive. She will put the same number of cans in each basket. She has 42 cans for the baskets. How many cans can she put in each basket?

Write the missing number in each number sentence.

2. _____ × 3 = 21

3. 5 × _____ = 25

4. 10 × 1 = _____

5. 2 × 4 = _____

6. 9 × _____ = 36

7. _____ × 6 = 18

8. For each expression in 8a–8d, answer Yes or No if the ☐ = 4 makes the number sentence true.

   a. 20 = ☐ × 4   YES   NO

   b. 8 × ☐ = 32   YES   NO

   c. 28 ÷ 7 = ☐   YES   NO

   d. 12 ÷ ☐ = 3   YES   NO

 3

9. Explain how to use multiplication to find the missing number in this number sentence.

$$\square \div 6 = 7.$$

Write the missing number in each equation.

10. _____ $\div 2 = 8$

11. $7 \div$ _____ $= 1$

12. $35 \div 5 =$ _____

13. $80 \div 10 =$ _____

14. $9 \div$ _____ $= 3$

15. _____ $\div 1 = 3$

16. For each expression in 16a–16d, answer Yes or No if the $\square = 7$ makes the number sentence true.

    a. $56 = \square \times 8$ YES   NO

    b. $\square \times 5 = 30$ YES   NO

    c. $63 \div 9 = \square$ YES   NO

    d. $24 \div \square = 3$ YES   NO

CC 8

Name _____

Common Core Standards Practice

3.OA.B.5 Apply properties of operations as strategies to multiply and divide.

1. For each expression in 1a–1d, answer Yes or No if the expression is equivalent to the product of 8 and 12.

   a. $8 \times (6 + 6)$ YES   NO

   b. $6 \times (8 + 6)$ YES   NO

   c. $(4 \times 2) + (6 \times 2)$ YES   NO

   d. $6 \times (4 + 4) + 6 \times (4 + 4)$ YES   NO

2. **a.** What is the missing number in the equation?

   $3 \times 10 = \underline{\hspace{1cm}} \times 3$

   b. Explain how you know.

3. **a.** What is one way to find $5 \times 2 \times 4$?

   b. What is another way to find $5 \times 2 \times 4$?

4. If you know that $5 \times 15 = 75$, how can you find 15×5?

5. You want to find $9 \times 2 \times 3$. Would you start by finding 9×2 or 2×3? Explain why.

6. Rosie wants to find 5×12. She breaks apart 12 into $10 + 2$. Then she writes $5 \times (10 + 2)$ as $(5 \times 10) + 2$.

   a. What mistake did Rosie make?

   b. What is 5×12? How do you know?

Name _____

Common Core Standards Practice

3.OA.B.6 Understand division as an unknown-factor problem.

Write a multiplication fact that can help you solve each division number sentence.

1. 12 ÷ 4 = ?

2. 35 ÷ 7 = ?

3. 7 ÷ 1 = ?

4. 36 ÷ 6 = ?

5. 25 ÷ 5 = ?

6. 27 ÷ 3 = ?

7. Which multiplication fact can you use to solve the division number sentence?

14 ÷ 7 = ☐

A 7 × 1 = 7

B 7 × 2 = 14

C 2 × 14 = 28

D 7 × 7 = 49

CC 11

8. What multiplication fact can you use to find $72 \div 8$?

9. What multiplication fact can you use to find $48 \div 6$?

10. What are two division number sentences you could solve by using the multiplication fact $7 \times 3 = 21$?

11. What are two division number sentences you could solve by using the multiplication fact $4 \times 8 = 32$?

12. Which division number sentence can you solve using the multiplication fact $10 \times 2 = 20$?

    A $10 \div 2 = ?$

    B $20 \div 2 = ?$

    C $10 \div 5 = ?$

    D $20 \div 5 = ?$

Name _____

Common Core Standards Practice

3.OA.C.7 Fluently multiply and divide within 100, using strategies such as the relationship between multiplication and division (e.g., knowing that $8 \times 5 = 40$, one knows $40 \div 5 = 8$) or properties of operations. By the end of Grade 3, know from memory all products of two one-digit numbers.

Solve.

1. $\begin{array}{r} 8 \\ \times\ 7 \\ \hline \end{array}$

2. $\begin{array}{r} 6 \\ \times\ 8 \\ \hline \end{array}$

3. $39 \div 3 =$ _____

4. $36 \div 9 =$ _____

5. $\begin{array}{r} 12 \\ \times\ 5 \\ \hline \end{array}$

6. $\begin{array}{r} 9 \\ \times\ 6 \\ \hline \end{array}$

7. $54 \div 6 =$ _____

8. $72 \div 8 =$ _____

9. $\begin{array}{r} 7 \\ \times\ 9 \\ \hline \end{array}$

10. $\begin{array}{r} 7 \\ \times\ 7 \\ \hline \end{array}$

11. $40 \div 5 =$ _____

12. $32 \div 4 =$ _____

Solve.

13.   5
   ×9

14.   7
   ×4

15. 42 ÷ 6 = _____

16. 72 ÷ 6 = _____

17.   9
   ×9

18.   12
  ×8

19. 60 ÷ 5 = _____

20. 90 ÷ 9 = _____

21.   5
  ×4

22.   11
  ×6

23. 77 ÷ 11 = _____

24. 48 ÷ 4 = _____

Name _____

Common Core Standards Practice

3.OA.D.8 Solve two-step word problems using the four operations. Represent these problems using equations with a letter standing for the unknown quantity. Assess the reasonableness of answers using mental computation and estimation strategies including rounding.

1. Jeremy bought 9 water bottles with a $20 bill. Each water bottle cost $2. How much change should Jeremy receive?

   a. Write an equation to match the problem. Use the letter *c* to stand for the missing number.

   b. Solve the problem. Explain how you found the answer.

2. Isabel and Hank build birdhouses. Isabel builds 3 birdhouses every day. Hank builds 2 birdhouses every day. How many birdhouses can they build in 5 days?

   a. Isabel says they can build 15 birdhouses in 5 days. Is her answer reasonable? Explain how you know.

   b. Write an equation to match the problem. Use the letter *b* to stand for the missing number.

   c. Solve the problem. Explain how you found the answer.

3. A box of light bulbs costs $5. Each box holds 4 light bulbs. How much money will Fran spend to buy 8 light bulbs?

    a. Write an equation to match the problem. Use the letter *m* to stand for the missing number.

    b. Solve the problem. Explain how you found the answer.

4. Jerome needs 65 balloons for a party. He already has 18 red balloons and 13 blue balloons. How many more balloons does Jerome need?

    a. Write an equation to match the problem. Use the letter *b* to stand for the missing number.

    b. Solve the problem. Explain how you found the answer.

    c. Explain how you could use an estimate to check that your answer is reasonable.

Name _____

Common Core Standards Practice

3.OA.D.9 Identify arithmetic patterns (including patterns in the addition table or multiplication table), and explain them using properties of operations.

1. Look at the numbers in the table. What pattern do you see?

2	5	8	11	14

Use the multiplication table for Problems 2 and 3.

X	0	1	2	3	4	5	6
0	0	0	0	0	0	0	0
1	0	1	2	3	4	5	6
2	0	2	4	6	8	10	12
3	0	3	6	9	12	15	18
4	0	4	8	12	16	20	24
5	0	5	10	15	20	25	30
6	0	6	12	18	24	30	36

2. Look at the row for 6 in the table. Explain why 6 times a number is always even.

3. Look at the row for 4 in the table. Explain why 4 times a number can be written as the sum of two equal addends.

4. Look at the numbers in the table. What pattern do you see?

7	14	21	28	35

Use the addition table for Problems 5 and 6.

+	1	2	3	4	5	6
1	2	3	4	5	6	7
2	3	4	5	6	7	8
3	4	5	6	7	8	9
4	5	6	7	8	9	10
5	6	7	8	9	10	11
6	7	8	9	10	11	12

5. Look at the row for 5 in the table. Explain why the numbers in this row follow the pattern even, odd, even, odd.

6. Explain why the sum of two equal addends is even.

Common Core Standards Practice

3.NBT.A.1 Use place value understanding to round whole numbers to the nearest 10 or 100.

Round each number to the nearest ten.

1. 118

2. 731

3. 1,552

4. 2,219

5. 6,382

6. 925

7. Which of these numbers, when rounded to the nearest 10, is 780? Circle all that round to 780.

784   789   773   776   758

8. Explain how to use place value to round 286 to the nearest 10.

Round each number to the nearest hundred.

9. 210

10. 2,547

11. 1,472

12. 889

13. 2,149

14. 7,975

15. Ryan says that 472 rounded to the nearest 10 is 500. Is Ryan correct? Explain.

16. Which of these is equal to 360? Circle all that are equal to 360.

4 × 90	80 × 4	12 × 30	40 × 9
50 × 7	6 × 60	40 × 8	5 × 60

Name _____

Common Core Standards Practice

3.NBT.A.2 Fluently add and subtract within 1000 using strategies and algorithms based on place value, properties of operations, and/or the relationship between addition and subtraction.

Add.

1. 237
  + 194

2. 359
  + 209

3. 808
  + 115

4. 556
  + 436

5. What is 438 + 194?

   A 522
   B 564
   C 622
   D 632

6. What is 703 + 167?

   A 800
   B 810
   C 860
   D 870

7. **a.** Find the sum. 243 + 239.

   b. Explain how you added 243 and 239.

Subtract.

8.
```
  320
-  16
```

9.
```
  334
-  53
```

10.
```
  289
- 122
```

11.
```
  901
- 576
```

12. What is 487 − 158?

   A 321

   B 329

   C 331

   D 339

13. What is 901 − 76?

   A 825

   B 835

   C 925

   D 975

14. Lilly says that 512 − 392 is 280.

   a. How can Lily use addition to check her answer?

   b. Explain how you know that Lily's answer is incorrect.

   c. What is the correct answer?

Name _____

Common Core Standards Practice

3.NBT.A.3 Multiply one-digit whole numbers by multiples of 10 in the range 10–90 (e.g., 9 × 80, 5 × 60) using strategies based on place value and properties of operations.

Multiply.

1. 7 × 20 = _____

2. 8 × 40 = _____

3. 9 × 60 = _____

4. 2 × 30 = _____

5. 6 × 70 = _____

6. 5 × 50 = _____

7. Explain how you can use 4 × 4 to help you find 4 × 40.

8. To find 8 × 70, Nora first wrote 70 as 7 × 10. Explain why this step can help Nora solve the problem.

9. Write the factors in the matching column. Some factors may not belong in any of the columns.

360	480	180

6 × 80   80 × 2   4 × 90   12 × 40

30 × 6   60 × 6   8 × 40   2 × 90

10. Match the factors with the products. Some products may have more than one set of factors. Some products may have no sets of factors.

3×70 80×3 5×50 12×20 40×6

210   240   250   270

11. A bookstore receives 7 boxes of books. Each box holds 20 books.

    a. Write a multiplication fact that shows how many books there are in all.

    b. Explain how you can use 7×2 to help solve the multiplication problem.

    c. How many books are there in all?

12. Anna multiplied 2×50 and got 10.

    a. Explain how you know that Anna's answer is incorrect.

    b. Explain how Anna could find the correct answer.

Name _____

Common Core Standards Practice

3.NF.A.1 Understand a fraction $\frac{1}{b}$ as the quantity formed by 1 part when a whole is partitioned into b equal parts; understand a fraction $\frac{a}{b}$ as the quantity formed by a parts of size $\frac{1}{b}$.

1. Lucy divided the circle into equal parts as shown.

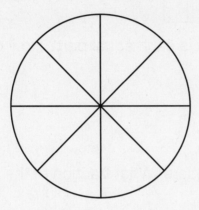

    a. How many equal parts does the circle have?

    b. Shade 5 parts of the circle.

    c. What fraction of the circle is shaded? Tell how you know.

2. Divide the circle into 4 equal parts. Then shade $\frac{1}{4}$.

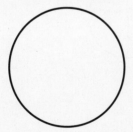

3. What fraction of the circle is shaded?

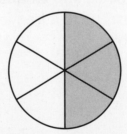

    A $\frac{1}{3}$

    B $\frac{3}{6}$

    C $\frac{1}{6}$

    D $\frac{3}{3}$

4. Look at the square below. It is divided into 4 equal parts.

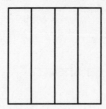

    a. What fraction of the square is each equal part? How do you know?

    b. Shade three parts of the square. What fraction of the square did you shade? How do you know?

5. a. Shade the circle to show $\frac{2}{3}$.

    b. Explain how you showed the fraction $\frac{2}{3}$.

6. Sean divided a circle into 2 equal parts. He shaded 1 part. Write a fraction to name the part Sean shaded.

Name _____

Common Core Standards Practice

3.NF.A.2a Understand a fraction as a number on the number line; represent fractions on a number line diagram.
a. Represent a fraction $\frac{1}{b}$ on a number line diagram by defining the interval from 0 to 1 as the whole and partitioning it into b equal parts. Recognize that each part has size $\frac{1}{b}$ and that the endpoint of the part based at 0 locates the number $\frac{1}{b}$ on the number line.

1. Ella divides the distance between 0 and 1 on a number line into 8 equal parts.

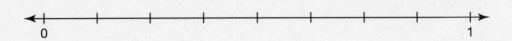

   a. What fraction names the size of each equal part?

   _____

   b. Draw and label the point on the number line that shows $\frac{1}{8}$.

2. Look at the point on the number line.

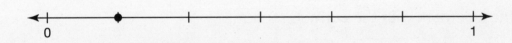

   a. What fraction does the point show?

   b. Explain how you know.

3. Divide the number line between 0 and 1 into four equal sections. Then draw and label a point to show $\frac{1}{4}$.

4. a. Draw and label a point to show $\frac{1}{3}$ on the number line.

0   1

b. Explain how you knew where to draw the point for $\frac{1}{3}$.

5. a. Divide the number line between 0 and 1 into 2 equal parts.

0   1

b. What fraction names the size of each equal part? _____

c. Label the tick mark with the correct fraction.

6. Alana makes a number line from 0 to 1. She uses tick marks to divide it into equal parts.

0   1

a. Write a fraction to label the first tick mark to the right of 0.

b. Explain how you knew which fraction to write.

Name _____

Common Core Standards Practice

3.NF.A.2b Understand a fraction as a number on the number line; represent fractions on a number line diagram.
b. Represent a fraction $\frac{a}{b}$ on a number line diagram by marking off a lengths $\frac{1}{b}$ from 0. Recognize that the resulting interval has size $\frac{a}{b}$ and that its endpoint locates the number $\frac{a}{b}$ on the number line.

1. Bridget divides a number line into eight equal parts.

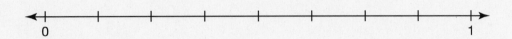

   a. Draw and label a point to show $\frac{5}{8}$.

   b. Explain how you knew where to draw the point for $\frac{5}{8}$.

2. Look at the letters on the number line.

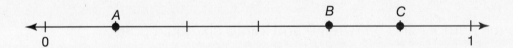

   Which letter on the number line shows $\frac{5}{6}$? Explain how you know.

3. Divide the number line between 0 and 1 into four equal parts. Then draw and label a point to show $\frac{2}{4}$.

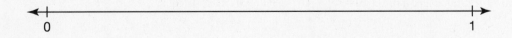

4. a. Draw and label a point to show $\frac{3}{4}$ on the number line.

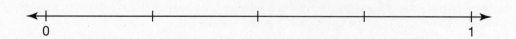

0   1

b. Explain how you knew where to draw the point for $\frac{3}{4}$.

5. a. Divide the number line between 0 and 1 into three equal parts.

0   1

b. What fraction names the size of each equal part? _____

c. Draw and label a point at $\frac{2}{3}$ on the number line.

6. a. Divide the number line between 0 and 1 into six equal parts.

0   1

b. Explain how you used tick marks to show sixths on the number line.

c. Draw and label a point to show $\frac{3}{6}$ on the number line.

CC 30

Name _____

Common Core Standards Practice

3.NF.A.3a Explain equivalence of fractions in special cases, and compare fractions by reasoning about their size. Understand two fractions as equivalent (equal) if they are the same size, or the same point on a number line.

1. a. Draw and label a point to show $\frac{1}{2}$ on the number line.

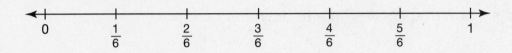

b. What fraction with a denominator of 6 is equal to $\frac{1}{2}$? How do you know?

2. a. Draw and label a point to show $\frac{1}{4}$ on the number line.

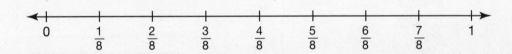

b. What fraction with a denominator of 8 is equal to $\frac{1}{4}$?

3. Grant shaded a circle to show $\frac{1}{2}$.

Grant's Circle   **Your Circle**

a. The circle on the right shows fourths. Shade it to show a fraction equal to $\frac{1}{2}$.

b. What fraction with a denominator of 4 is equal to $\frac{1}{2}$?

4. a. Draw and label a point to show $\frac{3}{4}$ on the number line.

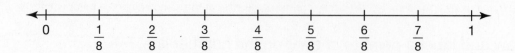

b. Explain how you knew where to draw the point for $\frac{3}{4}$.

c. What fraction with a denominator of 8 is equal to $\frac{3}{4}$?

5. Rachel shaded a circle to show $\frac{4}{6}$.

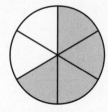

a. Shade the circle below to show a fraction equal to $\frac{4}{6}$.

b. What fraction of your circle is shaded?

6. Abby and Will each shaded a fraction of a rectangle.

Abby:

Will:

a. What fraction did Abby shade?

b. What fraction did Will shade?

c. Are the two fractions equal? How do you know?

Name _____

Common Core Standards Practice

3.NF.A.3b Explain equivalence of fractions in special cases, and compare fractions by reasoning about their size. Recognize and generate simple equivalent fractions, e.g., $\frac{1}{2} = \frac{2}{4}$, $\frac{4}{6} = \frac{2}{3}$. Explain why the fractions are equivalent, e.g., by using a visual fraction model.

1. Which model shows a fraction equivalent to $\frac{3}{6}$?

A

C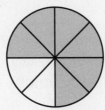

B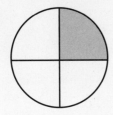

D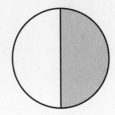

2. a. Which of these fractions are equivalent to $\frac{6}{8}$.

$\frac{4}{6}$ $\qquad$ $\frac{8}{12}$ $\qquad$ $\frac{2}{4}$ $\qquad$ $\frac{3}{4}$ $\qquad$ $\frac{9}{12}$

b. Draw models to show why the fractions are equivalent.

3. a. Name a fraction that is equivalent to $\frac{1}{3}$.

b. Explain why the fraction you named is equivalent to $\frac{1}{3}$. Use both words and a drawing.

CC 33

4. a. Which of these fractions are equivalent to $\frac{2}{8}$.

$\frac{3}{12}$ $\qquad$ $\frac{4}{12}$ $\qquad$ $\frac{1}{4}$ $\qquad$ $\frac{2}{4}$ $\qquad$ $\frac{3}{6}$

b. Draw models to show why the fractions are equivalent.

5. a. Which of these fractions are equivalent to $\frac{1}{2}$.

$\frac{4}{6}$ $\qquad$ $\frac{3}{6}$ $\qquad$ $\frac{2}{3}$ $\qquad$ $\frac{2}{4}$ $\qquad$ $\frac{4}{8}$

b. Use the number line to show why the fractions are equivalent.

6. a. Name a fraction that is equivalent to $\frac{4}{6}$.

b. Explain why the fraction you named is equivalent to $\frac{4}{6}$. Use both words and a drawing.

7. Miguel ate $\frac{2}{4}$ of an apple. April ate an equivalent fraction of an apple. Which could be the fraction that April ate?

A $\frac{2}{8}$

B $\frac{1}{3}$

C $\frac{3}{6}$

D $\frac{3}{4}$

Name _____

Common Core Standards Practice

3.NF.A.3c Explain equivalence of fractions in special cases, and compare fractions by reasoning about their size. Express whole numbers as fractions, and recognize fractions that are equivalent to whole numbers.

1. Which fraction is equal to 5?

 A $\frac{1}{5}$

 B $\frac{2}{5}$

 C $\frac{5}{1}$

 D $\frac{5}{5}$

2. Explain how to write the whole number 4 as a fraction.

3. Look at the number line.

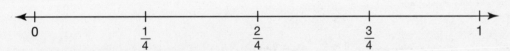

 a. Draw and label a point to show $\frac{4}{4}$.

 b. Explain how you knew where to draw the point for $\frac{4}{4}$.

4. Which letter on the number line shows $\frac{3}{3}$?

CC 35

5. Mari ate $\frac{2}{2}$ of a peach. What whole number of peaches did Mari eat?

   A 1 peach

   B 2 peaches

   C 3 peaches

   D 4 peaches

6. Which fraction is equal to the whole number 8?

   A $\frac{0}{8}$

   B $\frac{1}{8}$

   C $\frac{8}{1}$

   D $\frac{8}{8}$

7. Look at the number line.

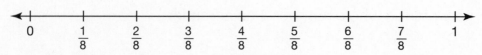

   a. Draw and label point to show $\frac{8}{8}$.

   b. Explain how you knew where to draw the point for $\frac{8}{8}$.

8. Ken wrote the whole number 10 as the fraction $\frac{10}{1}$. Did Ken write the correct fraction for the whole number 10? Explain.

9. Which letter on the number line shows $\frac{6}{6}$?

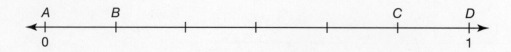

Name _____

Common Core Standards Practice

3.NF.A.3d Explain equivalence of fractions in special cases, and compare fractions by reasoning about their size. Compare two fractions with the same numerator or the same denominator by reasoning about their size. Recognize that comparisons are valid only when the two fractions refer to the same whole. Record the results of comparisons with the symbols >, =, or <, and justify the conclusions, e.g., by using a visual fraction model.

1. **a.** Which fraction is greater, $\frac{2}{6}$ or $\frac{4}{6}$?

    b. Explain how you know which fraction is greater.

2. Sadie ate $\frac{2}{8}$ of a small pizza. Josef ate $\frac{2}{8}$ of a large pizza. Did Sadie and Josef eat the same amount of pizza? Explain.

3. **a.** Which fraction is greater, $\frac{5}{8}$ or $\frac{5}{6}$?

    b. Explain how you know which fraction is greater.

4. Place the fractions below in the appropriate place.

Less than $\frac{1}{2}$	Equal to $\frac{1}{2}$	Greater than $\frac{1}{2}$

$\frac{3}{8}$ $\frac{4}{6}$ $\frac{2}{4}$ $\frac{5}{8}$ $\frac{1}{3}$

$\frac{5}{12}$ $\frac{2}{8}$ $\frac{6}{10}$ $\frac{3}{6}$ $\frac{7}{8}$

CC 37

5. Which fraction is less than $\frac{2}{6}$?

   A $\frac{2}{8}$

   B $\frac{2}{4}$

   C $\frac{3}{6}$

   D $\frac{5}{6}$

6. Circle the smaller fraction.

     $\frac{6}{8}$ $\frac{3}{8}$

7. Ben and Theo each have an orange. The oranges are the same size. Ben eats $\frac{2}{3}$ of his orange. Theo eats $\frac{2}{4}$ of his orange.

   a. Did Ben or Theo eat a larger fraction of the orange?

   b. Draw models of each fraction to show that your answer is correct.

8. a. Which fraction is larger, $\frac{1}{4}$ or $\frac{3}{4}$?

   b. Use the number line to show that your answer is correct.

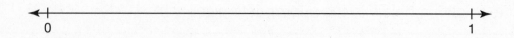

   0   1

9. Alonso painted $\frac{1}{2}$ of a large wall. Adele painted $\frac{1}{2}$ of a small wall. Do you think they used the same amount of paint? Explain.

Name _____

Common Core Standards Practice

3.MD.A.1 Tell and write time to the nearest minute and measure time intervals in minutes. Solve word problems involving addition and subtraction of time intervals in minutes, e.g., by representing the problem on a number line diagram.

1. Write the time shown on the clock.

_____ : _____

2. Alex leaves for school every day at 8:20. Show this time on the clock below.

3. After school each day, Devin spends 25 minutes on his math homework and 15 minutes on his language arts homework. How many minutes does Devin spend doing his math and language arts homework?

4. Laura goes to lunch at the time shown on the clock. At what time does she go to lunch?

_____ : _____

5. Lily and her parents drove to her grandmother's house. They arrived at her grandmother's house at 9:40 a.m. The drive took 45 minutes. At what time did Lily and her parents leave their house?

   a. Model this problem on the number line.

   b. Tell what time Lily and her parents left their house.

6. Tristan's math class starts at 1:37. Draw hands on the clock to show 1:37.

7. A play ended at 7:30. It began 1 hour and 10 minutes earlier. At what time did the play begin?

_____ : _____

8. What time does the clock show?

_____ : _____

9. After school, Marta and her sister play one game for 45 minutes. Then they play another game for 30 minutes. For how long did Marta and her sister play games?

10. Julia got on the bus at 2:20 P.M. She got off the bus 50 minutes later. At what time did she get off the bus?

a. Model this problem on the number line.

b. Tell what time Julie got off the bus.

Name _____

Common Core Standards Practice

3.MD.A.2 Measure and estimate liquid volumes and masses of objects using standard units of grams (g), kilograms (kg), and liters (l). Add, subtract, multiply, or divide to solve one-step word problems involving masses or volumes that are given in the same units, e.g., by using drawings (such as a beaker with a measurement scale) to represent the problem.

1. Which is the best estimate of the capacity of the pitcher?

   A 1 liter
   B 5 liters
   C 10 liters
   D 100 liters

2. Mr. Roberts went to the farmer's market on Wednesday and bought 450 grams of ground beef and 600 grams of ground pork. How much meat did Mr. Robert buy on Wednesday?

   A 250 grams
   B 510 grams
   C 1,050 grams
   D 1,150 grams

3. Circle the best estimate for the mass of the pillow.

   1 kg   10 kg   100 kg

4. A bathtub holds 150 liters of water. A sink holds 12 liters of water. How many more liters of water does the bathtub hold than the sink?

5. Ryan has 2 apples. One has a mass of 130 grams. The other has a mass of 124 grams. What is the combined mass of the two apples?

6. How many liters of water are in the bucket?

7. A bag of food has a mass of 20 kilograms. A worker at a zoo uses all of the food in the bag to feed 10 animals. She gives each animal an equal share of the food. How many kilograms of food does each animal get?

A 2 kilograms

B 10 kilograms

C 30 kilograms

D 200 kilograms

9. What is the mass of the tomatoes on the scale?

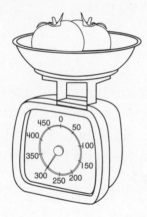

8. Circle the best estimate for the mass of the bowling ball.

400 kg   40 kg   4 kg

10. In science class, Ashton put 150 milliliters of oil in the beaker. Then he put 50 milliliters of vinegar into the same beaker.

a. On the beaker below, show the amount of oil and vinegar Ashton put in the beaker.

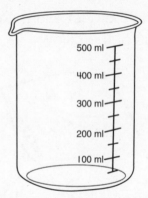

b. How many milliliters of liquid did Ashton put in the beaker?

11. Blanca bought 9 bottles of juice for a party. Each bottle holds 2 liters of juice. How many liters of juice did Blanca buy?

a. What operation do you need to use to solve the problem? Explain why?

b. How many liters of juice did Blanca buy?

Name _____

Common Core Standards Practice

3.MD.B.3 Draw a scaled picture graph and a scaled bar graph to represent a data set with several categories. Solve one- and two-step "how many more" and "how many less" problems using information presented in scaled bar graphs.

1. Use the information in the tally chart to complete the picture graph.

Favorite Sports of Third Graders

Sport	Tally
Baseball	~~IIII~~ I
Football	~~IIII~~ III
Soccer	~~IIII~~ ~~IIII~~ II

Favorite Sports of Third Graders

Baseball	
Football	
Soccer	
Key:	stands for 2 students

How many more students picked soccer as their favorite sport than baseball? Tell how you know.

The picture graph below shows how the third-grade students at a school get to school each day. Use the picture graph for questions 2 and 3.

Ways to Get to School

Bus	✪ ✪ ✪ ✪ ✪
Bike	✪
Walk	✪ ✪
Car	✪ ✪ ✪ ✪
Key: ✪ stands for 6 students	

2. How many fewer students walk to school than ride in a car?

3. How many more students take the bus to school than walk or bike?

4. The table shows the number of laps that 4 students swam last week. Use the information in the table to complete the bar graph.

Name	Laps
Molly	50
Fred	40
Jessica	45
Mateo	30

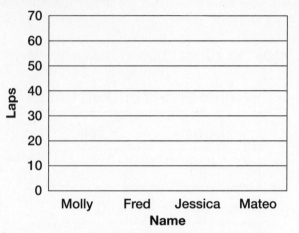

The bar graph below shows the number of some of the animals at a zoo. Use the bar graph for questions 5 and 6.

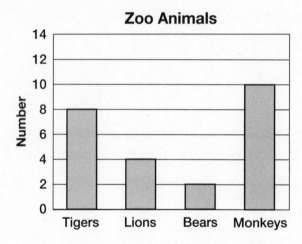

5. How many fewer bears than tigers are at the zoo?

6. Lions and tigers are large cats. How many more large cats than monkeys are at the zoo?

Name _____

Common Core Standards Practice

3.MD.B.4 Generate measurement data by measuring lengths using rulers marked with halves and fourths of an inch. Show the data by making a line plot, where the horizontal scale is marked off in appropriate units—whole numbers, halves, or quarters.

1. The list below shows the lengths of the snakes at a pet store. Display the data in a line plot.

Snake Lengths (inches)					
$6\frac{1}{2}$	7	$7\frac{1}{4}$	$6\frac{3}{4}$	$6\frac{3}{4}$	$7\frac{1}{2}$
$6\frac{3}{4}$	$6\frac{1}{2}$	$7\frac{1}{2}$	$7\frac{1}{4}$	$6\frac{3}{4}$	$7\frac{1}{4}$

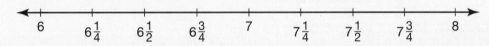

2. Find 6 pencils in your classroom.

   a. Use a ruler to measure each pencil to the nearest fourth of an inch. Write the length of each pencil below.

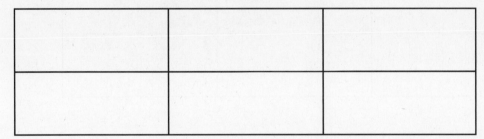

   b. Use the lengths of the pencils to complete the line plot.

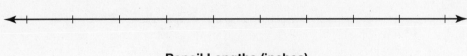

Pencil Lengths (inches)

3. The list below shows the lengths of Aaron's toy cars. Use the information to complete the line plot.

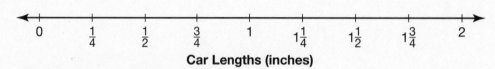

Car Lengths (inches)				
1	$1\frac{3}{4}$	2	$1\frac{1}{2}$	2
1	$1\frac{1}{2}$	2	2	1

Car Lengths (inches)

4. Find 6 crayons in your classroom.

   a. Use a ruler to measure each crayon to the nearest fourth of an inch. Write the length of each crayon below.

   b. Use the lengths of the crayons to complete the line plot.

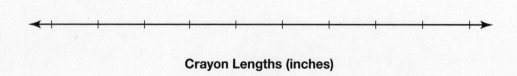

Crayon Lengths (inches)

Name _____

Common Core Standards Practice

3.MD.C.5a Recognize area as an attribute of plane figures and understand concepts of area measurement. A square with side length 1 unit, called "a unit square," is said to have "one square unit" of area, and can be used to measure area.
3.MD.C.5b Recognize area as an attribute of plane figures and understand concepts of area measurement. A plane figure which can be covered without gaps or overlaps by *n* unit squares is said to have an area of *n* square units.

1. Alicia is to find the area of this rectangle. She has some inch squares. Tell her what to do to find the area.

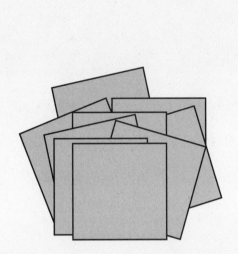 

2. Hudson completely covers a rectangle with unit squares as shown below. What is the area of the rectangle? How do you know?

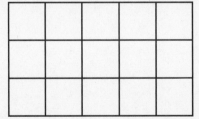

3. Which of these objects can Milly use to find the area of a square? Explain your answer.

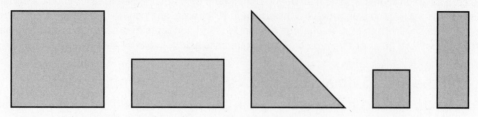

4. Cassie has a new rug in her bedroom. The rug is 9 square feet. Draw a model of Cassie's new rug. Show that it is 9 square feet.

5. Circle the units used to measure area.

feet	square inches	centimeters
square meters	square feet	meters

Name _____

Common Core Standards Practice

3.MD.C.6 Measure areas by counting unit squares (square cm, square m, square in, square ft, and improvised units).

1. What is the area of the rectangle below?

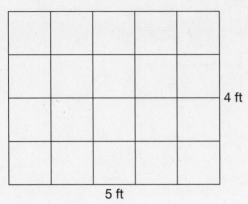

2. Explain how you found the area of the rectangle.

Find the area of each figure. Be sure to use the correct units.

3.

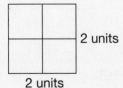

4.

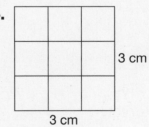

Find the area of each figure. Be sure to use the correct units.

5.

2 m

4 m

6.

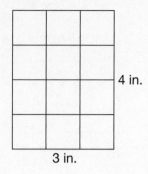

4 in.

3 in.

7. What is the area of the square shown below?

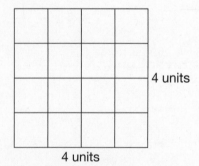

4 units

4 units

   A   4 square units

   B   8 square units

   C   12 square units

   D   16 square units

8. What is the area of the rectangle shown below?

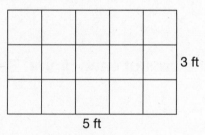

3 ft

5 ft

   A   8 square feet

   B   12 square feet

   C   15 square feet

   D   18 square feet

Name _____

Common Core Standards Practice

3.MD.C.7a Relate area to the operations of multiplication and addition. Find the area of a rectangle with whole-number side lengths by tiling it, and show that the area is the same as would be found by multiplying the side lengths.

Look at the rectangle on the grid.

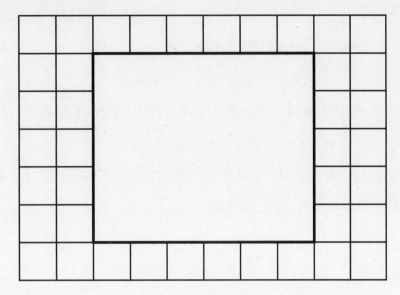

1. What is the area of the rectangle above? Tell how you know.

2. What is the length of the rectangle above? Tell how you determined the length.

3. What is the height of the rectangle above? Tell how you determined the height.

4. How does the product of the length and height relate to the number of squares that the rectangle covers?

5. Look at the rectangle below.

4 ft

2 ft

a. How many squares cover the rectangle?

b. Multiply the length and the width of the rectangle. What answer do you get?

c. What do you notice about the answers in part a and part b? What does that tell you about finding the area?

6. a. Give two different ways to find the area of the square.

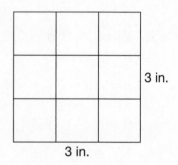

3 in.

3 in.

b. Use both ways to find the area of the square.

First way: Area =

Second way: Area =

c. Do you get the same answer? Why?

Name _____

Common Core Standards Practice

3.MD.C.7b Relate area to the operations of multiplication and addition. **b.** Multiply side lengths to find areas of rectangles with whole-number side lengths in the context of solving real world and mathematical problems, and represent whole-number products as rectangular areas in mathematical reasoning.

Find the area of each square or rectangle.

1.

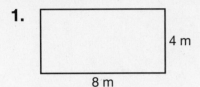

4 m

8 m

2.

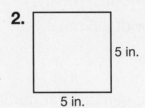

5 in.

5 in.

3. A rug is shaped like a rectangle. The length of the rug is 9 feet, and the width is 6 feet. What is the area of the rug?

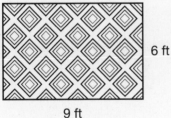

6 ft

9 ft

A 30 square ft

B 15 square ft

C 54 square ft

D 63 square ft

4. Ms. Leonard plans to put square tiles on her kitchen floor. Each tile covers 1 square foot and costs $1. How much will the tiles for the floor cost?

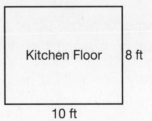

Kitchen Floor   8 ft

10 ft

5. Troy wants to make a pen for his rabbits. The pen will be a rectangle with an area of 24 square meters. Answer Yes or No if the length and width could be the dimensions of Troy's rabbit pen.

A length: 2 m, width: 6 m   YES   NO

B length: 3 m, width: 8 m   YES   NO

C length: 5 m, width: 5 m   YES   NO

D length: 4 m, width: 6 m   YES   NO

6. Izzie is planting a garden. Her garden is shaped like a rectangle. The length is 7 feet, and the width is 3 feet.

a. Draw a picture of Izzie's garden. Label the length and width.

b. What is the area of Izzie's garden?

Area =

7. The drawing shows the lid of a box. Lorrie is gluing square tiles to the lid. Each tile has an area of 1 square centimeter.

a. How many tiles will Lorrie need to completely cover the lid?

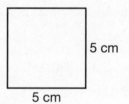

5 cm

5 cm

b. Explain how you found your answer.

Name _____

Common Core Standards Practice

3.MD.C.7c Relate area to the operations of multiplication and addition. Use tiling to show in a concrete case that the area of a rectangle with whole-number side lengths a and $b + c$ is the sum of $a \times b$ and $a \times c$. Use area models to represent the distributive property in mathematical reasoning.

1. Max drew a model of his garden. He has one part for vegetables and one part for herbs.

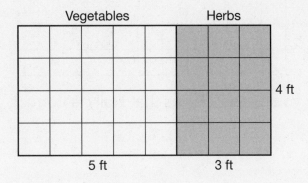

a. What is the area of the part of the garden for vegetables?

b. What is the area of the part of the garden for herbs?

c. What is the area of the garden?

2. Ralph's father will put new tiles on the kitchen floor. Ralph draws a model of the kitchen floor. What is the area of the kitchen floor?

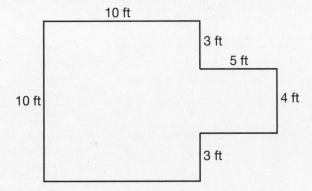

3. Holly says that 3 × 9 is the same as the sum of 3 × 5 and 3 × 4.

    a. On the grid below, draw a model to show that Holly is correct.

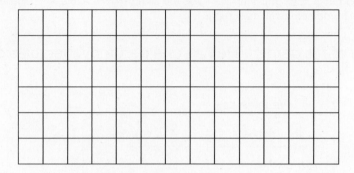

    b. Explain how your model shows that Holly is correct.

4. How does the model below show that 7 × 7 is the same as (7 × 5) + (7 × 2)?

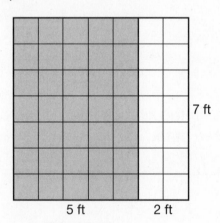

7 ft

5 ft   2 ft

Name _____

Common Core Standards Practice

3.MD.C.7d Relate area to the operations of multiplication and addition. Recognize area as additive. Find areas of rectilinear figures by decomposing them into non-overlapping rectangles and adding the areas of the non-overlapping parts, applying this technique to solve real world problems.

1. Linda's bedroom floor has side lengths of 12 feet and 9 feet. She drew a picture of the floor, and then broke it apart into two smaller rectangles.

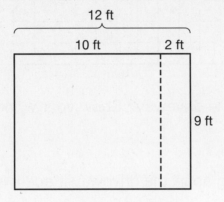

   a. What is the area of each smaller rectangle?

   b. What is the total area of the floor? How do you know?

2. Curt made a bookmark in the shape of a rectangle. The bookmark has a length of 15 centimeters and a width of 5 centimeters.

   a. Break apart the bookmark into two smaller rectangles to make it easier to find the area.

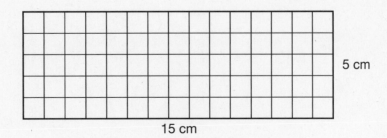

   b. What is the area of the bookmark? Show your work.

3. A driveway has the shape of a rectangle. It is 16 meters long and 4 meters wide.

   a. Break apart the driveway into two smaller rectangles to make it easier to find the area.

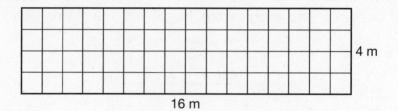

16 m

4 m

   b. What is the area of the driveway? Show your work.

   c. Explain how breaking apart the driveway made it easier to find the area.

4. A mirror has the shape of a rectangle. It is 13 inches long and 6 inches wide. What is the area of the mirror? Show your work.

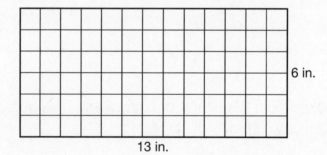

6 in.

13 in.

Name _____

Common Core Standards Practice

3.MD.D.8 Solve real world and mathematical problems involving perimeters of polygons, including finding the perimeter given the side lengths, finding an unknown side length, and exhibiting rectangles with the same perimeter and different areas or with the same area and different perimeters.

1. Harry's father is building a tree house. The model below represents the floor. What will be the perimeter of the floor?

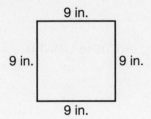

Perimeter = _____

2. Ama is making a banner. The model below represents her banner. She will put gold cord around the banner. How many centimeters of gold cord will she use?

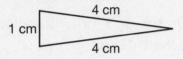

Perimeter = _____

3. The perimeter of the triangle is 9 centimeters. What is the missing side length?

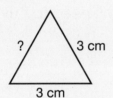

4. The perimeter of the figure is 20 inches. What is the missing side length?

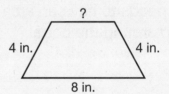

5. The drawing shows the yard of the Lang family. What is the perimeter of the yard?

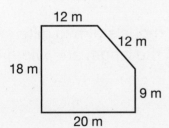

6. Look at the rectangle shown below.

    a. What are the perimeter and area of the rectangle?

       Perimeter = _____   Area = _____

    b. On the grid, draw a rectangle that has the same perimeter, but a different area.

    c. What is the area of the rectangle you drew?

7. A farmer needs to build a new animal corral in the shape of a rectangle. The pen needs to have an area of 72 square meters. He will need to buy fencing to go around the corral.

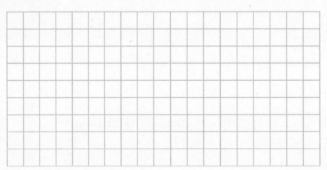

    a. What could be the dimensions of the corral? Draw models of two different rectangles with an area of 72 square meters. Label the length and width of each model.

    b. Which of your models will require more fencing? Tell how you know.

Common Core Standards Practice

3.G.A.1 Understand that shapes in different categories (e.g., rhombuses, rectangles, and others) may share attributes (e.g., having four sides), and that the shared attributes can define a larger category (e.g., quadrilaterals). Recognize rhombuses, rectangles, and squares as examples of quadrilaterals, and draw examples of quadrilaterals that do not belong to any of these subcategories.

1. What are two ways these shapes are alike?

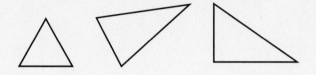

2. Circle the shapes that have 4 sides and exactly 2 right angles.

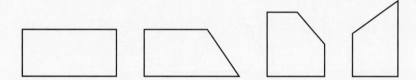

3. Which of these shapes appears to be a rhombus?

A    C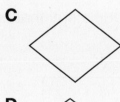

B 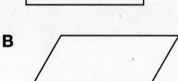   D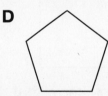

4. Which of these quadrilaterals is NOT a rectangle?

A 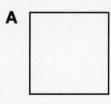   C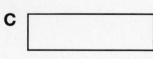

B    D

5. a. Draw a quadrilateral that is not a rhombus, a square, or a rectangle.

b. Explain how you know that your quadrilateral is not a rhombus, a square, or a rectangle.

6. What is one way these shapes are alike?

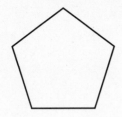  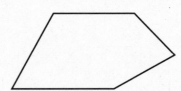

7. a. Circle the quadrilateral that appears to be a square.

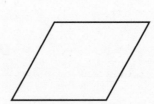 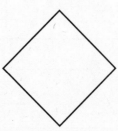

b. Explain how you know that the quadrilateral you picked is a square.

Name _____

Common Core Standards Practice

3.G.A.2 Partition shapes into parts with equal areas. Express the area of each part as a unit fraction of the whole.

1. The rectangle is divided into 4 equal parts. What fraction of the area of the rectangle is the area of each part?

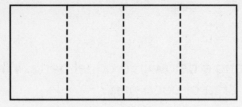

   A $\frac{1}{4}$ **C** $\frac{1}{2}$

   B $\frac{1}{3}$ **D** $\frac{3}{4}$

2. Look at the hexagon.

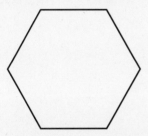

   a. Divide the hexagon into 6 equal parts.

   b. What fraction of the area of the hexagon is the area of each part?

3. **a.** Show three different ways you can divide a square into 2 equal parts.

   b. What fraction of the area of the square is the area of each part?

4. Look at the circle.

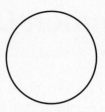

    a. Divide the circle into equal parts so that the area of each part is $\frac{1}{4}$ of the area of the circle.

    b. Into how many equal parts did you divide the circle?

5. Brian divided the rectangle below into equal parts. What fraction of the area of the rectangle is the area of each part?

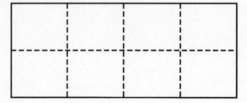

6. Ella divided a triangle into 3 parts as shown below.

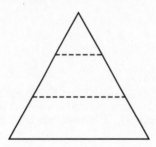

    a. Ella says that the area of each part is $\frac{1}{3}$ of the area of the triangle. Explain why Ella is incorrect.

    b. Divide the triangle below into 3 parts so that the area of each part is $\frac{1}{3}$ of the total area.

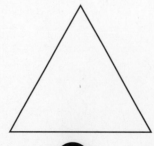

Name _____

Practice End-of-Year Assessment

1. The bar graph shows the favorite pets of the third grade.

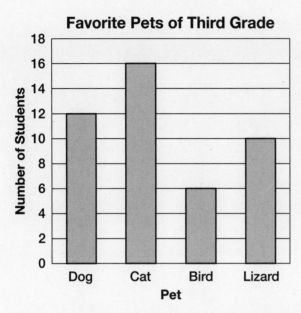

How many more students chose dogs or cats than chose birds?

....

2. **a.** Name a fraction equivalent to $\frac{1}{4}$.

   b. Draw models to show why the fractions are equivalent.

3. Sara buys 6 pencils with a $20 bill. Each pencil costs $2.

   a. How much change should Sara receive?

   b. Explain how you found your answer.

---

4. Which of these numbers round to 1,780 when rounded to the nearest ten? Circle all that apply.

1,784	1,874	1,775
1,708	1,779	1,799

---

5. There are 3 rows of cans. Each row has 4 cans.

   a. Draw an array to show how many cans there are in all.

   b. How many cans are there in all?

6. Divide the number line into three equal parts. Then draw and label a point to show $\frac{1}{3}$.

0   1

7. Which multiplication facts can you use to solve the division problem? Circle all that apply.

$24 \div 6 = \boxed{}$

$1 \times 6 = 6$ $2 \times 12 = 24$ $4 \times 6 = 24$

$6 \times 6 = 36$ $6 \times 4 = 24$ $3 \times 8 = 24$

8. a. Divide the number line into 4 equal parts. Draw and label a point to show $\frac{1}{4}$ on the number line.

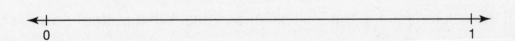

0   1

b. Explain how you knew where to draw the point for $\frac{1}{4}$.

9. Compare the fractions. Write >, =, or <.

$$\frac{1}{5} \underline{\hspace{2cm}} \frac{1}{9}$$

Explain how you know which fraction is greater. Draw a model to support your explanation.

....

10. For which of these equations is 3 the missing factor? Circle all that apply.

$6 \times \boxed{} = 18$ 　　 $\boxed{} \times 4 = 16$ 　　 $8 \times \boxed{} = 16$

$7 \times \boxed{} = 21$ 　　 $\boxed{} \times 9 = 27$ 　　 $3 \times \boxed{} = 12$

....

11. Look at the column for 4 in the multiplication table. What pattern do you see?

X	0	1	2	3	4	5	6
0	0	0	0	0	0	0	0
1	0	1	2	3	4	5	6
2	0	2	4	6	8	10	12
3	0	3	6	9	12	15	18
4	0	4	8	12	16	20	24
5	0	5	10	15	20	25	30
6	0	6	12	18	24	30	36

12. Leo needs 4 pieces of tape, each 5 inches long.

    a. Write an equation to show how much tape Leo needs in all. Use the letter *t* to stand for the missing number.

    b. How many inches of tape does Leo need in all?

---

13. Baseball practice ended at 4:10. It began 30 minutes earlier. Which shows when baseball practice began?

    A 3:40

    B 3:10

    C 4:40

    D 3:50

---

14. Tell how to find 4×9 by breaking apart 9 into $5 + 4$. You can use words or models.

15. A cook makes 3 pots of soup. Each pot holds 8 liters of soup. How many liters of soup did the cook make in all?

16. Look at the numbers in the table. What pattern do you see?

4	9	14	19	24

17. There are 28 people going on a boat ride. Each boat can hold 4 people.

    a. Write an equation to show how many boats they will need. Use the letter *b* to stand for the missing number.

    b. How many boats will they need?

18. What is the area of the rectangle? Be sure to use the correct units.

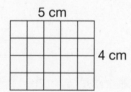

5 cm

4 cm

19. A fish has a mass of 26 kilograms. The mass of a turtle is 8 kilograms less than the mass of the fish. What is the mass of the turtle?

....

20. **a.** What is the missing number in the equation?

$$9 \times 8 = \boxed{} \times 9$$

b. Explain how you know.

....

21. **a.** Write a word problem that matches $12 \div 4$.

b. Explain why your problem matches $12 \div 4$.

22. A third grade class is growing bean plants. The list below shows the heights of the plants. Use the information to complete the line plot.

Plant Heights (inches)				
$7\frac{1}{2}$	6	$6\frac{1}{4}$	7	$6\frac{3}{4}$
$6\frac{1}{4}$	7	$7\frac{1}{2}$	7	$6\frac{3}{4}$

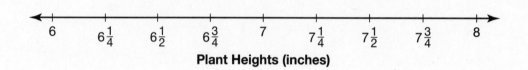

6    $6\frac{1}{4}$ $6\frac{1}{2}$ $6\frac{3}{4}$ 7 $7\frac{1}{4}$ $7\frac{1}{2}$ $7\frac{3}{4}$ 8

Plant Heights (inches)

....

23. For which of these equations is the missing value equal to 7? Circle all that apply.

$63 \div 9 = \boxed{}$ $56 \div \boxed{} = 7$ $27 \div \boxed{} = 3$

$54 \div 6 = \boxed{}$ $35 \div 5 = \boxed{}$ $49 \div \boxed{} = 7$

....

24. Write the time shown on the clock.

_____ : _____

25. **a.** Divide the figure into 8 equal parts. Then shade one of the parts.

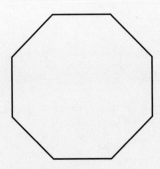

   b. What fraction of the area of the figure is the area of the shaded part?

26. What is the area of the rectangle?

3 units

4 units

27. Which number makes the equation true?

$$48 \div \boxed{} = 8$$

A 8

B 7

C 6

D 9

28. The perimeter of the figure is 18 feet.

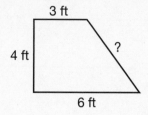

a. What is the missing side length?

b. Tell how you know.

---

29. For each equation in 29a–29d, answer Yes or No if the ☐ = 8 makes the equation true.

a. 4 × ☐ = 32   YES   NO

b. ☐ × 6 = 56   YES   NO

c. 5 × ☐ = 40   YES   NO

d. ☐ × 8 = 56   YES   NO

---

30. Ms. Carr has a flowerbed in the shape of a rectangle. The flowerbed has a length of 14 feet and a width of 4 feet.

a. Break apart the flowerbed into two smaller rectangles to make it easier to find the area.

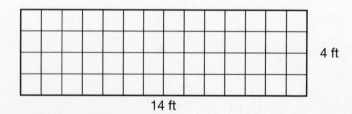

b. What is the area of the flowerbed? Show your work.

31. How can the product of 6 and 7 help you find the product of 60 and 7?

....

32. Write a multiplication fact that can help you solve the division problem.

$36 \div 9 = \boxed{}$

....

33. A door is shaped liked a rectangle. The length of the door is 7 feet, and the width is 3 feet. What is the area of the door?

7 ft

3 ft

34. a. Divide the rectangle into 3 equal parts. Shade 1 of the parts.

b. What fraction of the rectangle is shaded?

....

35. Which quadrilateral does NOT have any square corners?

A

C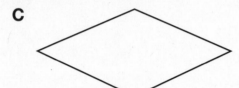

B

D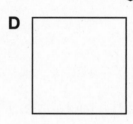

....

36. A flag has an area of 12 square feet. Explain what this sentence means.

37. Multiply.

$$\begin{array}{r} 9 \\ \times\ 5 \\ \hline \end{array}$$

....

38. Erin had 28 cards. She kept 8 for herself. She shared the rest equally between her 2 brothers.

a. How many cards did each of Erin's brothers get?

b. Explain how you found your answer.

....

39. Subtract.

$$\begin{array}{r} 326 \\ -\ \ 38 \\ \hline \end{array}$$

....

40. Mr. Padilla has 3 apples. He cuts each apple into 8 pieces. He puts 4 apple pieces into each bag.

a. How many bags will Mr. Padilla need?

b. Explain how you found your answer.

Name _____

Performance Task 1
Raising Funds

Part A

The students in Ms. Jansen's third grade class are having a school bake sale. They want to raise $500 for a fieldtrip.

Ms. Jansen asked her students' families to volunteer to bring in brownies, cookies, or large cupcakes for the sale.

From the volunteer sign-up sheets, Ms. Jansen determines they will have 80 large cupcakes and 240 brownies for the bake sale. Nobody signed up to bring in cookies yet.

The students decide that they will sell the large cupcakes for $2 each, and brownies and cookies for $1 each.

1. How much money can the students make if they sell all of the cupcakes and brownies?

2. How many cookies will be needed for the class to reach their goal of $500?

3. How many families will need to volunteer to bring cookies, if each family brings 20 cookies?

Part B

The bake sale will take place from 11:00 to 12:00 every school day for one week. The students will set up tables outside the school lunchroom and will invite teachers, students, and parents to the bake sale.

Ms. Jansen has decided to have 30-minute shifts for the bake sale. Two students will work at each shift.

4. How many shifts will each of the 20 students in the class have to work during the week-long bake sale?

Performance Task 2

A Nature Hike

Part A

Colton and Rashad are hiking a trail to a waterfall in a nature preserve. After hiking for 30 minutes, they see the sign below.

Rashad says, "Half-way? Is that all? That's less than $\frac{1}{3}$ of the trail."

Colton disagrees. He says, "$\frac{1}{2}$ of the trail is greater than $\frac{1}{3}$ of the trail."

1. Who is correct? Use two different models to show whether Rashad or Colton is correct.

Part B

Colton and Rashad each have a water bottle for the hike. When they began the hike, their water bottles were full. Their water bottles are shown below.

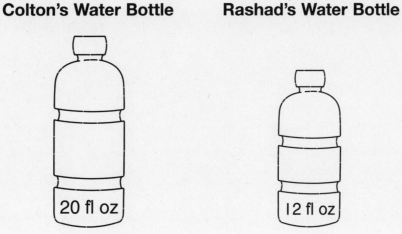

Colton's Water Bottle   **Rashad's Water Bottle**

20 fl oz   12 fl oz

When they get to the waterfall, Colton says, "My water bottle is half empty."

Rashad looks at his water bottle and says, "Mine is, too. But you have more water left than I do." Colton answers, "How can I have more water? Both of our bottles are half empty."

2. Why does Rashad say that Colton has more water left in his bottle than he does?

3. How can Rashad show Colton that he is correct? Explain what Rashad can do.

Name _____

Practice End-of-Year Assessment
Test 2

1. The picture graph shows the favorite snacks of the third grade.

Favorite Snacks of Third Grade

Food	Number of Students
Apples	☺ ☺ ☺
Carrots	☺ ☺
Crackers	☺ ☺ ☺ ☺
Peanuts	☺

Key: ☺ stands for 2 students

How many fewer students chose carrots than chose crackers?

....

2. **a.** Name a fraction equivalent to $\frac{3}{6}$.

b. Draw models to show why the fractions are equivalent.

CC 83

3. Abby has 2 boxes of crayons. Each box holds 8 crayons. Abby gives 6 of her crayons to her sister.

    a. How many crayons does Abby have left?

    b. Explain how you found your answer.

---

4. Which of these numbers round to 3500 when rounded to the nearest hundred? Circle all that apply.

    3482   3561   3550

    3450   3409   3490

---

5. Blake makes 6 rows of stamps. Each row has 3 stamps.

    a. Draw an array to show how many stamps there are in all.

    b. How many stamps are there in all?

6. Divide the number line into two equal parts. Then draw and label a point to show $\frac{1}{2}$.

0   1

7. Which multiplication facts can you use to solve the division problem?

$8 \div 2 = \boxed{}$

$1 \times 8 = 8$ $2 \times 2 = 4$ $2 \times 4 = 8$

$4 \times 2 = 8$ $2 \times 8 = 16$ $8 \times 2 = 16$

8. a. Draw and label a point to show $\frac{1}{6}$ on the number line.

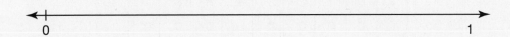

0   1

b. Explain how you knew where to draw the point for $\frac{1}{6}$.

9. Compare the fractions. Write >, =, or <.

$$\frac{1}{6} \underline{\hspace{2cm}} \frac{1}{3}$$

Explain how you know which fraction is greater. Draw a model to support your explanation.

....

10. For which of these equations is 7 the missing factor? Circle all that apply.

$3 \times \boxed{} = 21$ $\boxed{} \times 5 = 30$ $6 \times \boxed{} = 42$

$7 \times \boxed{} = 47$ $\boxed{} \times 4 = 28$ $\boxed{} \times 8 = 54$

....

11. Look at the column for 8 in the multiplication table. What pattern do you see?

X	0	1	2	3	4	5	6	7	8
0	0	0	0	0	0	0	0	0	0
1	0	1	2	3	4	5	6	7	8
2	0	2	4	6	8	10	12	14	16
3	0	3	6	9	12	15	18	21	24
4	0	4	8	12	16	20	24	28	32
5	0	5	10	15	20	25	30	35	40
6	0	6	12	18	24	30	36	42	48
7	0	7	14	21	28	35	42	49	56
8	0	8	16	24	32	40	48	56	64

CC 86

12. Hal is helping his father build a wooden support for their garden. They will use 8 boards of wood that are each 4 feet long.

    a. Write an equation that can be used to find how many feet of boards Hal and his father will use. Use the letter *r* to stand for the missing number.

    b. How many feet of wood will they use?

....

13. Leah finished her homework at 7:10. She started her homework 40 minutes earlier. At what time did Leah start her homework?

_____ : _____

....

14. Tell how to find 3 × 8 by breaking apart 8 into 5 + 3. You can use words or models.

15. Nancy is helping to clean the class fish tank. She needs to put 24 liters of water in the tank. The bucket she is using holds 4 liters. How many buckets full of water will she need to fill the tank?

....

16. Look at the numbers in the table. What pattern do you see?

5	9	13	17	21

....

17. A town has 40 baseballs for its 5 baseball teams. Each team will get the same number of baseballs.

a. Write an equation to show how many baseballs each team will get. Use the letter *b* to stand for the missing number.

b. How many baseballs will each team get?

....

18. What is the area of the rectangle? Be sure to use the correct units.

9 cm

3 cm

19. A box holds 4 bags of sand. The total mass of all 4 bags is 32 kilograms. Each bag has the same mass. What is the mass of each bag?

20. **a.** What is the missing number in the equation?

$$2 \times 7 = \boxed{} \times 2$$

b. Explain how you know.

21. **a.** Write a word problem that matches $25 \div 5$.

b. Explain why your problem matches $25 \div 5$.

22. The list below shows the lengths of several leaves from a tree. Use the information to complete the line plot.

Lengths of Leaves (inches)				
$1\frac{3}{4}$	1	$2\frac{3}{4}$	3	$2\frac{1}{2}$
$1\frac{1}{2}$	$1\frac{1}{2}$	$1\frac{3}{4}$	$1\frac{1}{2}$	$1\frac{3}{4}$

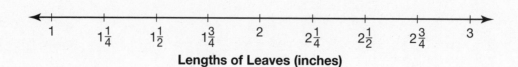

Lengths of Leaves (inches)

....

23. For which of these equations is the missing value equal to 9? Circle all that apply.

$63 \div 7 = \boxed{}$ $40 \div 5 = \boxed{}$ $45 \div 5 = \boxed{}$

$16 \div 2 = \boxed{}$ $36 \div 4 = \boxed{}$ $90 \div 9 = \boxed{}$

....

24. Write the time shown on the clock.

_____ : _____

25. a. Divide the figure into 6 equal parts. Then shade one of the parts.

b. What fraction of the area of the figure is the area of the shaded part?

26. What is the area of the rectangle?

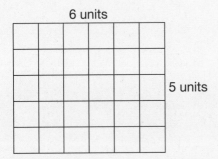

6 units

5 units

27. Which number makes the equation true?

$$63 \div \boxed{} = 9$$

A 6

B 7

C 8

D 9

28. a. What is the perimeter of the figure?

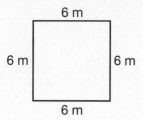

6 m

6 m   6 m

6 m

b. Tell how you found the perimeter.

---

29. For each equation in 29a–29d, answer Yes or NO if the ⬚ = 6 makes the equation true.

a. $3 \times$ ⬚ $= 18$ YES   NO

b. $4 \times$ ⬚ $= 28$ YES   NO

c. ⬚ $\times 5 = 30$ YES   NO

d. ⬚ $\times 8 = 46$ YES   NO

---

30. The bottom of a pan is shaped like a rectangle. The pan has a length of 11 inches and a width of 7 inches.

a. Break apart the bottom of the pan into two smaller rectangles to make it easier to find the area.

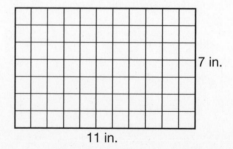

7 in.

11 in.

b. What is the area of the bottom of the pan? Show your work.

31. Explain how you can use 2 × 3 to help you find 2 × 30.

....

32. Write a multiplication fact that can help you solve the division problem.

42 ÷ 6 = ☐

....

33. A pool is shaped liked a rectangle. The length of the pool is 10 meters, and the width is 8 meters. What is the area of the pool?

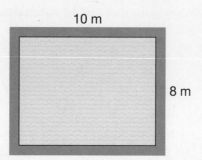

10 m

8 m

34. a. Divide the figure into 8 equal parts. Shade 1 of the parts.

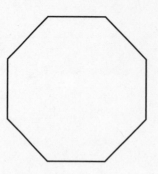

b. What fraction of the figure is shaded?

35. Which figure is not a quadrilateral?

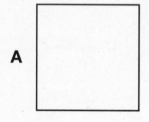

A

B

C

D

36. A napkin has an area of 36 square inches. Explain what this sentence means.

37. Multiply.

$$\begin{array}{r} 8 \\ \times\ 8 \\ \hline \end{array}$$

---

38. Oliver had $14. He used some of the money to buy 5 pencils. Now Oliver has $4 left.

   a. How much did each pencil cost?

   b. Explain how you found your answer.

---

39. Add.

$$\begin{array}{r} 338 \\ +\ 457 \\ \hline \end{array}$$

---

40. Five friends have 35 tickets. They share the tickets equally. Hannah is one of the friends. She gives away 3 of her tickets.

   a. How many tickets does Hannah have left?

   b. Explain how you found your answer.

Name _____

Performance Task 3

Town Pride

Part A

Students from a local elementary school have volunteered to help get their town ready for its 200th anniversary celebration. Eight students, led by Madeleine, will paint a wall that is on one side of the town hall and library. The wall they will paint is 28 feet long and 4 feet high. Each of the eight students on Madeleine's team will paint an equal part of the wall. A model of the wall is shown below.

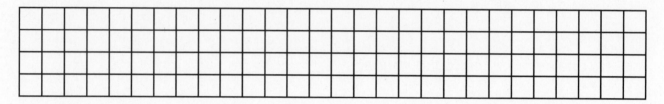

1. How can Madeleine divide up the wall into equal sections for the 8 students on her team?

2. What will be the size of the section that each student will paint? Explain how you found your answer.

Part B

A second group was going to paint another wall that is 16 feet long by 4 feet high. At the last minute, the group was assigned to a different project, so Madeleine's team will paint this wall, too.

A model of the wall is shown below.

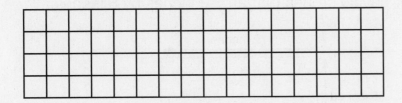

3. How can Madeleine divide up the two walls into equal sections for the 8 students in her team? (Hint: Think about whether all team members paint sections of both walls.)

4. What is the total number of square feet each team member will paint? Explain how you know.

Performance Task 4

Paving Stones

Part A

Tami's father wants to build a patio in their back yard. The patio will be 60 inches long and 36 inches wide. He will use paving stones. He will use paving stones that are 9-inch square or paving stones that are 12 inches by 6 inches.

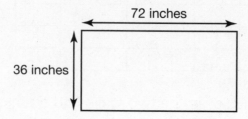

72 inches

36 inches

1. Which paving stone should Tami's father use if he wants to use the fewest number of paving stones? Explain your answer using models.

Part B

The 9-inch square paving stones cost $3 for each paving stone. The 12-inch by 6-inch paving stones are on sale for $2 for each paving stone.

2. Which paving stone should Tami's father use if he wants to spend the least amount for the paving stones? How much will he save? Explain your answer using models or equations.

Answers and Rubrics

Page CC 1

Name _____

Common Core Standards Practice

3.OA.A.1 Interpret products of whole numbers, e.g., interpret 5 × 7 as the total number of objects in 5 groups of 7 objects each.

1. Molly has 3 packs of pencils. Each pack holds 8 pencils. Molly writes 3 × 8 to represent the problem situation. What does 3 × 8 show?

the total number of pencils Molly has

2. There are 5 kittens. Each kitten has 4 legs. What expression can represent the total number of legs?

5 × 4

3. Write a problem story that matches 7 × 3.

Possible answer: Allie is making dolls. Each doll needs 3 buttons. How many buttons does Allie need to make 7 dolls?

4. Explain why your story matches 7 × 3.

Possible answer: 7 × 3 is the total number of buttons in 7 groups of 3 buttons each.

page CC 1

Page CC 2

5. Write a word problem story that matches 3 × 5.

Possible answer: Holly puts 5 towels in each of 3 boxes. How many towels does Holly have in all?

6. Explain why your story matches 3 × 5.

Possible answer: 3 × 5 is the total number of towels in 3 groups of 5 towels each.

7. Brad planted 6 rows of flowers. He planted 4 flowers in each row. Tell why 6 × 4 gives the total number of flowers Brad planted.

There are 6 rows, so there are 6 groups. There are 4 flowers in each row, so there are 4 in each group. 6 × 4 is the number of flowers in 6 groups of 4 flowers each.

8. Marco buys 4 bags of apples. There are 10 apples in each bag. Tell why 4 × 10 gives the total number of apples.

There are 4 bags, so there are 4 groups. There are 10 apples in each bag, so there are 10 in each group. 4 × 10 is the number of apples in 4 groups of 10 apples each.

page CC 2

Page CC 3

Name _____

Common Core Standards Practice

3.OA.A.2 Interpret whole-number quotients of whole numbers, e.g., interpret 56 ÷ 8 as the number of objects in each share when 56 objects are partitioned equally into 8 shares, or as a number of shares when 56 objects are partitioned into equal shares of 8 objects each.

1. Sally is putting 32 muffins on 8 plates. Each plate has the same number of muffins. What expression shows how many muffins are on each plate?

32 ÷ 8

2. Jon has 24 oranges. He puts 6 oranges in each bag. What expression shows how many bags John needs?

24 ÷ 6

3. Write a problem story that matches 42 ÷ 7.

Possible answer: Seven friends are sharing 42 trading cards. Each friend gets the same number of cards. How many cards does each friend get?

4. Explain why your problem matches 42 ÷ 7.

Possible answer: 42 ÷ 7 gives the number of cards in each share when 42 cards are divided into 7 equal shares.

page CC 3

Page CC 4

5. Write a problem story that matches 27 ÷ 3.

Possible answer: Inez has 27 comic books. She puts 3 comic books in each bag. How many bags does Inez need?

6. Explain why your problem story matches 27 ÷ 3.

Possible answer: 27 ÷ 3 gives the number of shares when 27 comic books are divided into equal shares of 3 comic books each.

7. There are 56 students sitting at 8 tables. Each table has the same number of students. What expression can tell the number of students at each table.

56 ÷ 8

8. Ruben wants to buy 18 tennis balls. There are 3 balls in each can. What expression can tell the number of cans Ruben will need to buy?

18 ÷ 3

page CC 4

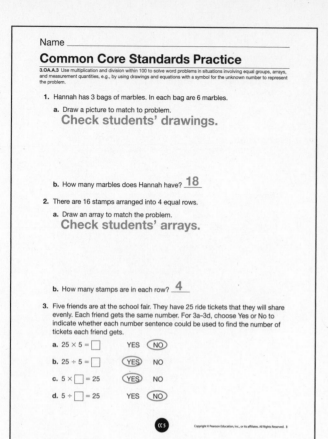

page CC 5

Common Core Standards Practice

3.OA.A.3 Use multiplication and division within 100 to solve word problems in situations involving equal groups, arrays, and measurement quantities, e.g., by using drawings and equations with a symbol for the unknown number to represent the problem.

1. Hannah has 3 bags of marbles. In each bag are 6 marbles.

   a. Draw a picture to match to problem.
   Check students' drawings.

   b. How many marbles does Hannah have? __18__

2. There are 16 stamps arranged into 4 equal rows.

   a. Draw an array to match the problem.
   Check students' arrays.

   b. How many stamps are in each row? __4__

3. Five friends are at the school fair. They have 25 ride tickets that they will share evenly. Each friend gets the same number. For 3a–3d, choose Yes or No to indicate whether each number sentence could be used to find the number of tickets each friend gets.

   a. $25 \times 5 = \square$ YES   (NO)

   b. $25 \div 5 = \square$ (YES)   NO

   c. $5 \times \square = 25$ (YES)   NO

   d. $5 \div \square = 25$ YES   (NO)

page CC 6

4. Ms Donovan sets up her classroom with 4 rows of desks. Each row has 5 desks.

   a. Draw an array to show how many desks Mrs. Donovan has in her classroom.
   Check students' drawings.

   b. How many desks are there in all? __20__

5. Sherri has 24 inches of yarn. She cuts the yarn into pieces that are each 6 inches long.

   a. Write an equation to show how many pieces of yarn Sherri has.
   Possible answer: 24 ÷ 6 = ?

   b. How many pieces of yarn does Sherri have? __4__

6. Roger's father has 6 pieces of wood. Each piece is 8 inches long. For 6a–6d, choose Yes or No to indicate whether each number sentence could be used to find how many inches of wood Roger's father has.

   a. $8 \times 6 = \square$ (YES)   NO

   b. $8 \div 6 = \square$ YES   (NO)

   c. $\square \times 6 = 8$ YES   (NO)

   d. $\square \div 6 = 8$ (YES)   NO

page CC 7

Common Core Standards Practice

3.OA.A.4 Determine the unknown whole number in a multiplication or division equation relating three whole numbers.

1. Write a multiplication number sentence to match this story problem.

   Maddy needs to fill 6 baskets with canned goods for the food drive. She will put the same number of cans in each basket. She has 42 cans for the baskets. How many cans can she put in each basket?

   $6 \times \boxed{} = 42$

Write the missing number in each number sentence.

2. $\underline{7} \times 3 = 21$

3. $5 \times \underline{5} = 25$

4. $10 \times 1 = \underline{10}$

5. $2 \times 4 = \underline{8}$

6. $9 \times \underline{4} = 36$

7. $\underline{3} \times 6 = 18$

8. For each expression in 8a–8d, answer Yes or No if the $\square$ = 4 makes the number sentence true.

   a. $20 = \square \times 4$ YES   (NO)

   b. $8 \times \square = 32$ (YES)   NO

   c. $28 \div 7 = \square$ (YES)   NO

   d. $12 \div \square = 3$ (YES)   NO

page CC 8

9. Explain how to use multiplication to find the missing number in this number sentence.

   $\square \div 6 = 7.$

   Possible answer: You can use the multiplication fact 7 × 6 = 42 to find the division fact 42 ÷ 6 = 7. So, the missing number is 42.

Write the missing number in each equation.

10. $\underline{16} \div 2 = 8$

11. $7 \div \underline{7} = 1$

12. $35 \div 5 = \underline{7}$

13. $80 \div 10 = \underline{8}$

14. $9 \div \underline{3} = 3$

15. $\underline{3} \div 1 = 3$

16. For each expression in 16a–16d, answer Yes or No if the $\square$ = 7 makes the number sentence true.

   a. $56 = \square \times 8$ (YES)   NO

   b. $\square \times 5 = 30$ YES   (NO)

   c. $63 \div 9 = \square$ (YES)   NO

   d. $24 \div \square = 3$ YES   (NO)

page CC 9

Name _____

Name _____

Common Core Standards Practice

3.OA.B.5 Apply properties of operations as strategies to multiply and divide.

1. For each expression in 1a–1d, answer Yes or No if the expression is equivalent to the product of 8 and 12.

   a. $8 \times (6 + 6)$ (YES)   NO

   b. $6 \times (8 + 6)$ YES   (NO)

   c. $(4 \times 2) + (6 \times 2)$ YES   (NO)

   d. $6 \times (4 + 4) + 6 \times (4 + 4)$ (YES)   NO

2. **a.** What is the missing number in the equation?

   $3 \times 10 = \underline{10} \times 3$

   b. Explain how you know.

   Possible answer: You can multiply numbers in any order. The product will stay the same. So, 3×10 is the same as 10×3.

3. **a.** What is one way to find $5 \times 2 \times 4$?

   Possible answer: First, multiply 5×2 to get 10. Then multiply 10×4 to get 40.

   b. What is another way to find $5 \times 2 \times 4$?

   Possible answer: First, multiply 2×4 to get 8. Then multiply 5×8 to get 40.

page CC 9

page CC 10

4. If you know that $5 \times 15 = 75$, how can you find 15×5?

   Possible answer: You can multiply two numbers in any order and the product will be the same. So, 15×5 is the same as 5×15. I know that $5 \times 15 = 75$, so $15 \times 5 = 75$.

5. You want to find $9 \times 2 \times 3$. Would you start by finding 9×2 or 2×3? Explain why.

   Possible answer: I would find 2×3 first. If I find 9×2 first, I then have to find 18×3. If I find 2×3 first, I then have to find 9×6. It is easier to find 9×6 than to find 18×3.

6. Rosie wants to find 5×12. She breaks apart 12 into $10 + 2$. Then she writes $5 \times (10 + 2)$ as $(5 \times 10) + 2$.

   a. What mistake did Rosie make?

   She forgot to multiply 2 and 5.

   b. What is 5×12? How do you know?

   60; Possible answer: I know that $5 \times 10 = 50$ and $5 \times 2 = 10$. So, $(5 \times 10) + (5 \times 2) = 50 + 10 = 60$.

page CC 10

page CC 11

Name _____

Common Core Standards Practice

3.OA.B.6 Understand division as an unknown-factor problem.

Write a multiplication fact that can help you solve each division number sentence.

1. $12 \div 4 = ?$
   $4 \times 3 = 12$ or $3 \times 4 = 12$

2. $35 \div 7 = ?$
   $5 \times 7 = 35$ or $7 \times 5 = 35$

3. $7 \div 1 = ?$
   $7 \times 1 = 7$ or $1 \times 7 = 7$

4. $36 \div 6 = ?$
   $6 \times 6 = 36$

5. $25 \div 5 = ?$
   $5 \times 5 = 25$

6. $27 \div 3 = ?$
   $3 \times 9 = 27$ or $9 \times 3 = 27$

7. Which multiplication fact can you use to solve the division number sentence?

   $14 \div 7 = \square$

   A $7 \times 1 = 7$
   (B) $7 \times 2 = 14$
   C $2 \times 14 = 28$
   D $7 \times 7 = 49$

page CC 11

page CC 12

8. What multiplication fact can you use to find $72 \div 8$?

   $8 \times 9 = 72$ or $9 \times 8 = 72$

9. What multiplication fact can you use to find $48 \div 6$?

   $6 \times 8 = 48$ or $8 \times 6 = 48$

10. What are two division number sentences you could solve by using the multiplication fact $7 \times 3 = 21$?

    $21 \div 3 = ?$ and $21 \div 7 = ?$

11. What are two division number sentences you could solve by using the multiplication fact $4 \times 8 = 32$?

    $32 \div 4 = ?$ and $32 \div 8 = ?$

12. Which division number sentence can you solve using the multiplication fact $10 \times 2 = 20$?

    A $10 \div 2 = ?$
    (B) $20 \div 2 = ?$
    C $10 \div 5 = ?$
    D $20 \div 5 = ?$

page CC 12

Page CC 13

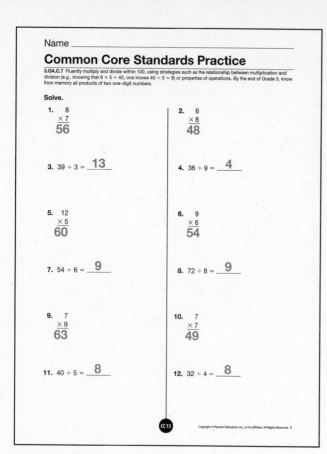

Name _____

Common Core Standards Practice

3.OA.C.7 Fluently multiply and divide within 100, using strategies such as the relationship between multiplication and division (e.g., knowing that 8 × 5 = 40, one knows 40 ÷ 5 = 8) or properties of operations. By the end of Grade 3, know from memory all products of two one-digit numbers.

Solve.

1. $\begin{array}{r} 8 \\ \times 7 \\ \hline 56 \end{array}$

2. $\begin{array}{r} 6 \\ \times 8 \\ \hline 48 \end{array}$

3. $39 \div 3 = \underline{13}$

4. $36 \div 9 = \underline{4}$

5. $\begin{array}{r} 12 \\ \times 5 \\ \hline 60 \end{array}$

6. $\begin{array}{r} 9 \\ \times 6 \\ \hline 54 \end{array}$

7. $54 \div 6 = \underline{9}$

8. $72 \div 8 = \underline{9}$

9. $\begin{array}{r} 7 \\ \times 9 \\ \hline 63 \end{array}$

10. $\begin{array}{r} 7 \\ \times 7 \\ \hline 49 \end{array}$

11. $40 \div 5 = \underline{8}$

12. $32 \div 4 = \underline{8}$

page CC 13

Page CC 14

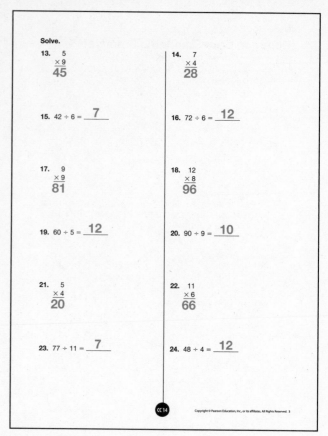

Solve.

13. $\begin{array}{r} 5 \\ \times 9 \\ \hline 45 \end{array}$

14. $\begin{array}{r} 7 \\ \times 4 \\ \hline 28 \end{array}$

15. $42 \div 6 = \underline{7}$

16. $72 \div 6 = \underline{12}$

17. $\begin{array}{r} 9 \\ \times 9 \\ \hline 81 \end{array}$

18. $\begin{array}{r} 12 \\ \times 8 \\ \hline 96 \end{array}$

19. $60 \div 5 = \underline{12}$

20. $90 \div 9 = \underline{10}$

21. $\begin{array}{r} 5 \\ \times 4 \\ \hline 20 \end{array}$

22. $\begin{array}{r} 11 \\ \times 6 \\ \hline 66 \end{array}$

23. $77 \div 11 = \underline{7}$

24. $48 \div 4 = \underline{12}$

page CC 14

Page CC 15

Name _____

Common Core Standards Practice

3.OA.D.8 Solve two-step word problems using the four operations. Represent these problems using equations with a letter standing for the unknown quantity. Assess the reasonableness of answers using mental computation and estimation strategies including rounding.

1. Jeremy bought 9 water bottles with a $20 bill. Each water bottle cost $2. How much change should Jeremy receive?

    a. Write an equation to match the problem. Use the letter c to stand for the missing number.

    Possible answer: $20 - (9 \times 2) = c$

    b. Solve the problem. Explain how you found the answer.
    Jeremy should receive $2 in change. Check students' explanations.

2. Isabel and Hank build birdhouses. Isabel builds 3 birdhouses every day. Hank builds 2 birdhouses every day. How many birdhouses can they build in 5 days?

    a. Isabel says they can build 15 birdhouses in 5 days. Is her answer reasonable? Explain how you know.
    No. Possible explanation: Isabel can build 15 birdhouses in 5 days without including Hank's birdhouses.

    b. Write an equation to match the problem. Use the letter b to stand for the missing number.
    Possible answer: $5 \times (3 + 2) = b$

    c. Solve the problem. Explain how you found the answer.
    They can build 25 birdhouses. Check students' explanations.

page CC 15

Page CC 16

3. A box of light bulbs costs $5. Each box holds 4 light bulbs. How much money will Fran spend to buy 8 light bulbs?

    a. Write an equation to match the problem. Use the letter m to stand for the missing number.

    Possible answer: $(8 \div 4) \times 5 = m$

    b. Solve the problem. Explain how you found the answer.
    Fran will spend $10. Check students' explanations.

4. Jerome needs 65 balloons for a party. He already has 18 red balloons and 13 blue balloons. How many more balloons does Jerome need?

    a. Write an equation to match the problem. Use the letter b to stand for the missing number.

    Possible answer: $65 - (18 + 13) = b$

    b. Solve the problem. Explain how you found the answer.
    Jerome needs 34 more balloons. Check students' explanations.

    c. Explain how you could use an estimate to check that your answer is reasonable.
    Possible answer: I can round each number to the nearest 10. The number 65 rounds to 70, 18 rounds to 20, and 13 rounds to 10. My estimate is $70 - (20 + 10) = 70 - 30 = 40$. The estimate is close to my answer of 34, so my answer is reasonable.

page CC 16

page CC 17

Name _____

Common Core Standards Practice

3.OA.D.9 Identify arithmetic patterns (including patterns in the addition table or multiplication table), and explain them using properties of operations.

1. Look at the numbers in the table. What pattern do you see?

2	5	8	11	14

Possible answer: Each number is 3 more than the number before it.

Use the multiplication table for Problems 2 and 3.

X	0	1	2	3	4	5	6
0	0	0	0	0	0	0	0
1	0	1	2	3	4	5	6
2	0	2	4	6	8	10	12
3	0	3	6	9	12	15	18
4	0	4	8	12	16	20	24
5	0	5	10	15	20	25	30
6	0	6	12	18	24	30	36

2. Look at the row for 6 in the table. Explain why 6 times a number is always even.

Possible answer: The row for 6 starts with the even number 0. Each number is 6 more than the number before it. When you add 6 to an even number, you get another even number.

3. Look at the row for 4 in the table. Explain why 4 times a number can be written as the sum of two equal addends.

Possible answer: The table shows that 4 times a number is always even. You can write an even number as 2 times a number. You can then write 2 times a number as the sum of two equal addends.

---

page CC 18

4. Look at the numbers in the table. What pattern do you see?

7	14	21	28	35

Possible answer: Each number is 7 more than the number before it.

Use the addition table for Problems 5 and 6.

+	1	2	3	4	5	6
1	2	3	4	5	6	7
2	3	4	5	6	7	8
3	4	5	6	7	8	9
4	5	6	7	8	9	10
5	6	7	8	9	10	11
6	7	8	9	10	11	12

5. Look at the row for 5 in the table. Explain why the numbers in this row follow the pattern even, odd, even, odd.

Possible answer: Each number is 1 more than the number before it. When you add 1 to an even number, you get an odd number. When you add 1 to an odd number, you get an even number.

6. Explain why the sum of two equal addends is even.

Possible answer: You can write the sum of two equal addends as 2 times a number. The product of 2 and a number is always even.

---

page CC 19

Name _____

Common Core Standards Practice

3.NBT.A.1 Use place value understanding to round whole numbers to the nearest 10 or 100.

Round each number to the nearest ten.

1. 118
   120

2. 731
   730

3. 1,552
   1,550

4. 2,219
   2,220

5. 6,382
   6,380

6. 925
   930

7. Which of these numbers, when rounded to the nearest 10, is 780? Circle all that round to 780.

   (784)　789　773　(776)　758

8. Explain how to use place value to round 286 to the nearest 10.

   Look at the ones place. The digit in the ones place is greater than 5, so add 1 to the digit in the tens place. Then write a 0 in the ones place. 286 rounded to the nearest 10 is 290.

---

page CC 20

Round each number to the nearest hundred.

9. 210
   200

10. 2,547
    2,500

11. 1,472
    1,500

12. 889
    900

13. 2,149
    2,100

14. 7,975
    8,000

15. Ryan says that 472 rounded to the nearest 10 is 500. Is Ryan correct? Explain.

    Yes. Ryan rounded to the nearest 100 instead of the nearest 10. The number 472 rounded to the nearest 10 is 470.

16. Which of these is equal to 360? Circle all that are equal to 360.

    (4×90)　80×4　(12×30)　(40×9)
    50×7　(6×60)　40×8　5×60

page CC 21

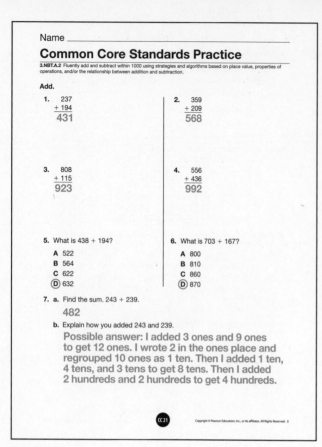

Common Core Standards Practice

3.NBT.A.2 Fluently add and subtract within 1000 using strategies and algorithms based on place value, properties of operations, and/or the relationship between addition and subtraction.

Add.

1. 237
    + 194
    ‾‾‾‾
    431

2. 359
    + 209
    ‾‾‾‾
    568

3. 808
    + 115
    ‾‾‾‾
    923

4. 556
    + 436
    ‾‾‾‾
    992

5. What is 438 + 194?
   A 522
   B 564
   C 622
   Ⓓ 632

6. What is 703 + 167?
   A 800
   B 810
   C 860
   Ⓓ 870

7. a. Find the sum. 243 + 239.
      482
   b. Explain how you added 243 and 239.
      Possible answer: I added 3 ones and 9 ones to get 12 ones. I wrote 2 in the ones place and regrouped 10 ones as 1 ten. Then I added 1 ten, 4 tens, and 3 tens to get 8 tens. Then I added 2 hundreds and 2 hundreds to get 4 hundreds.

page CC 22

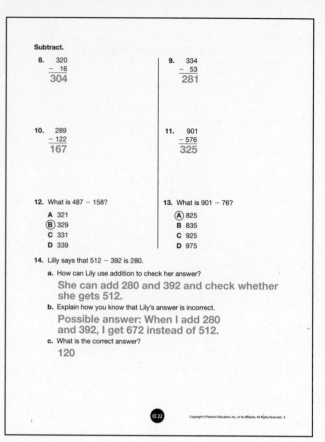

Subtract.

8. 320
    − 16
    ‾‾‾‾
    304

9. 334
    − 53
    ‾‾‾‾
    281

10. 289
     − 122
     ‾‾‾‾
     167

11. 901
     − 576
     ‾‾‾‾
     325

12. What is 487 − 158?
    A 321
    Ⓑ 329
    C 331
    D 339

13. What is 901 − 76?
    Ⓐ 825
    B 835
    C 925
    D 975

14. Lilly says that 512 − 392 is 280.
    a. How can Lilly use addition to check her answer?
       She can add 280 and 392 and check whether she gets 512.
    b. Explain how you know that Lilly's answer is incorrect.
       Possible answer: When I add 280 and 392, I get 672 instead of 512.
    c. What is the correct answer?
       120

page CC 23

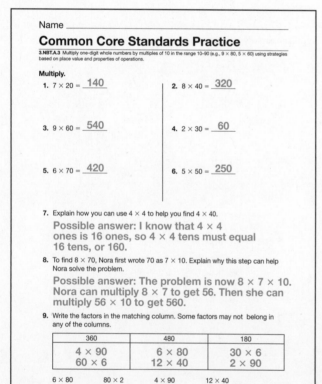

Common Core Standards Practice

3.NBT.A.3 Multiply one-digit whole numbers by multiples of 10 in the range 10–90 (e.g., 9 × 80, 5 × 60) using strategies based on place value and properties of operations.

Multiply.

1. 7 × 20 = __140__

2. 8 × 40 = __320__

3. 9 × 60 = __540__

4. 2 × 30 = __60__

5. 6 × 70 = __420__

6. 5 × 50 = __250__

7. Explain how you can use 4 × 4 to help you find 4 × 40.
   Possible answer: I know that 4 × 4 ones is 16 ones, so 4 × 4 tens must equal 16 tens, or 160.

8. To find 8 × 70, Nora first wrote 70 as 7 × 10. Explain why this step can help Nora solve the problem.
   Possible answer: The problem is now 8 × 7 × 10. Nora can multiply 8 × 7 to get 56. Then she can multiply 56 × 10 to get 560.

9. Write the factors in the matching column. Some factors may not belong in any of the columns.

360	480	180
4 × 90	6 × 80	30 × 6
60 × 6	12 × 40	2 × 90

6 × 80	80 × 2	4 × 90	12 × 40
30 × 6	60 × 6	8 × 40	2 × 90

page CC 24

10. Match the factors with the products. Some products may have more than one set of factors. Some products may have no sets of factors.

3 × 70	80 × 3	5 × 50	12 × 20	40 × 6

210	240	250	270

11. A bookstore receives 7 boxes of books. Each box holds 20 books.
    a. Write a multiplication fact that shows how many books there are in all.
       7 × 20
    b. Explain how you can use 7 × 2 to help solve the multiplication problem.
       Possible answer: I know that 7 × 2 ones is 14 ones, so 7 × 2 tens must equal 14 tens, or 140.
    c. How many books are there in all?
       140 books

12. Anna multiplied 2 × 50 and got 10.
    a. Explain how you know that Anna's answer is incorrect.
       Possible answer: I know that 2 × 5 = 10, so 2 × 50 must be greater than 10.
    b. Explain how Anna could find the correct answer.
       Possible answer: She can write 2 × 50 as 2 × 5 × 10. Next, multiply 2 × 5 to get 10. Then multiply 10 × 10 to get 100.

page CC 25

Name _____

Common Core Standards Practice

3.NF.A.1 Understand a fraction $\frac{1}{b}$ as the quantity formed by 1 part when a whole is partitioned into b equal parts; understand a fraction $\frac{a}{b}$ as the quantity formed by a parts of size $\frac{1}{b}$.

1. Lucy divided the circle into equal parts as shown.

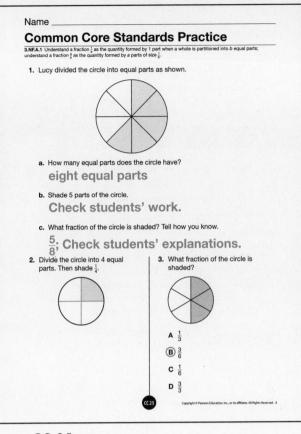

   a. How many equal parts does the circle have?

   eight equal parts

   b. Shade 5 parts of the circle.

   Check students' work.

   c. What fraction of the circle is shaded? Tell how you know.

   $\frac{5}{8}$; Check students' explanations.

2. Divide the circle into 4 equal parts. Then shade $\frac{1}{4}$.

3. What fraction of the circle is shaded?

   A $\frac{1}{3}$

   Ⓑ $\frac{3}{6}$

   C $\frac{1}{6}$

   D $\frac{3}{3}$

---

page CC 26

4. Look at the square below. It is divided into 4 equal parts.

   a. What fraction of the square is each equal part? How do you know?

   $\frac{1}{4}$; There are 4 equal parts, so each part is $\frac{1}{4}$ of the square.

   b. Shade three parts of the square. What fraction of the square did you shade? How do you know?

   $\frac{3}{4}$; Each equal part is $\frac{1}{4}$, and there are 3 parts shaded.

5. a. Shade the circle to show $\frac{2}{3}$.

   b. Explain how you showed the fraction $\frac{2}{3}$.

   The circle is divided into 3 equal parts. Each part is $\frac{1}{3}$, so I shaded 2 of the parts.

6. Sean divided a circle into 2 equal parts. He shaded 1 part. Write a fraction to name the part Sean shaded.

   $\frac{1}{2}$

---

page CC 27

Name _____

Common Core Standards Practice

3.NF.A.2a Understand a fraction as a number on the number line; represent fractions on a number line diagram.
a. Represent a fraction $\frac{1}{b}$ on a number line diagram by defining the interval from 0 to 1 as the whole and partitioning it into b equal parts. Recognize that each part has size $\frac{1}{b}$ and that the endpoint of the part based at 0 locates the number $\frac{1}{b}$ on the number line.

1. Ella divides the distance between 0 and 1 on a number line into 8 equal parts.

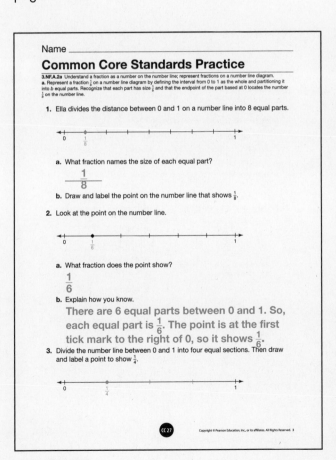

   a. What fraction names the size of each equal part?

   $\frac{1}{8}$

   b. Draw and label the point on the number line that shows $\frac{1}{8}$.

2. Look at the point on the number line.

   a. What fraction does the point show?

   $\frac{1}{6}$

   b. Explain how you know.

   There are 6 equal parts between 0 and 1. So, each equal part is $\frac{1}{6}$. The point is at the first tick mark to the right of 0, so it shows $\frac{1}{6}$.

3. Divide the number line between 0 and 1 into four equal sections. Then draw and label a point to show $\frac{1}{4}$.

---

page CC 28

4. a. Draw and label a point to show $\frac{1}{3}$ on the number line.

   b. Explain how you knew where to draw the point for $\frac{1}{3}$.

   There are 3 equal parts between 0 and 1. So, each equal part is $\frac{1}{3}$. To show $\frac{1}{3}$, I drew a point at the first tick mark to the right of 0.

5. a. Divide the number line between 0 and 1 into 2 equal parts.

   b. What fraction names the size of each equal part? **$\frac{1}{2}$**

   c. Label the tick mark with the correct fraction.

6. Alana makes a number line from 0 to 1. She uses tick marks to divide it into equal parts.

   a. Write a fraction to label the first tick mark to the right of 0.

   b. Explain how you knew which fraction to write.

   There are 5 equal parts between 0 and 1. So, each equal part is $\frac{1}{5}$. This means that the first tick mark to the right of 0 shows $\frac{1}{5}$.

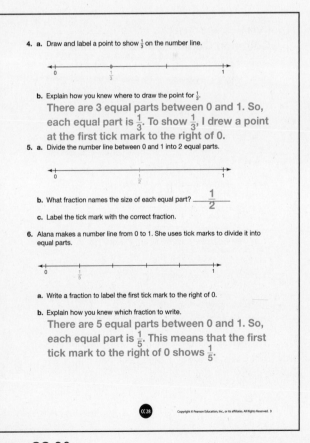

---

page CC 29

Name _____

Common Core Standards Practice

3.NF.A.2b Understand a fraction as a number on the number line; represent fractions on a number line diagram.
b. Represent a fraction $\frac{a}{b}$ on a number line diagram by marking off a lengths $\frac{1}{b}$ from 0. Recognize that the resulting interval has size $\frac{a}{b}$ and that its endpoint locates the number $\frac{a}{b}$ on the number line.

1. Bridget divides a number line into eight equal parts.

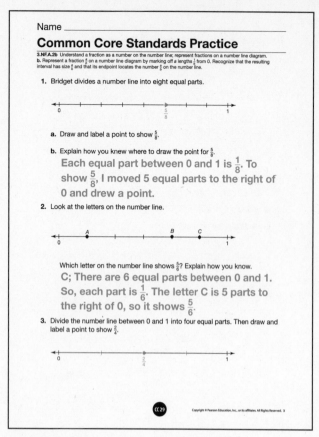

a. Draw and label a point to show $\frac{5}{8}$.

b. Explain how you knew where to draw the point for $\frac{5}{8}$.

Each equal part between 0 and 1 is $\frac{1}{8}$. To show $\frac{5}{8}$, I moved 5 equal parts to the right of 0 and drew a point.

2. Look at the letters on the number line.

Which letter on the number line shows $\frac{5}{6}$? Explain how you know.

C; There are 6 equal parts between 0 and 1. So, each part is $\frac{1}{6}$. The letter C is 5 parts to the right of 0, so it shows $\frac{5}{6}$.

3. Divide the number line between 0 and 1 into four equal parts. Then draw and label a point to show $\frac{2}{4}$.

CC 29   Copyright © Pearson Education, Inc., or its affiliates. All Rights Reserved. 3

---

page CC 30

4. a. Draw and label a point to show $\frac{3}{4}$ on the number line.

b. Explain how you knew where to draw the point for $\frac{3}{4}$.

There are 4 equal parts between 0 and 1. So, each equal part is $\frac{1}{4}$. To show $\frac{3}{4}$, I moved 3 equal parts to the right of 0 and drew a point.

5. a. Divide the number line between 0 and 1 into three equal parts.

b. What fraction names the size of each equal part? _____ $\frac{1}{3}$

c. Draw and label a point at $\frac{2}{3}$ on the number line.

6. a. Divide the number line between 0 and 1 into six equal parts.

b. Explain how you used tick marks to show sixths on the number line.

I used tick marks to divide the distance between 0 and 1 into 6 equal parts. Each equal part is $\frac{1}{6}$.

c. Draw and label a point to show $\frac{3}{6}$ on the number line.

CC 30   Copyright © Pearson Education, Inc., or its affiliates. All Rights Reserved. 3

---

page CC 31

Name _____

Common Core Standards Practice

3.NF.A.3a Explain equivalence of fractions in special cases, and compare fractions by reasoning about their size. Understand two fractions as equivalent (equal) if they are the same size, or the same point on a number line.

1. a. Draw and label a point to show $\frac{1}{2}$ on the number line.

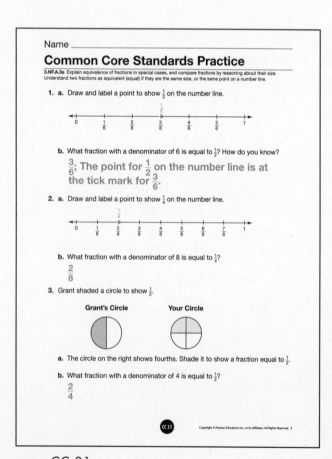

b. What fraction with a denominator of 6 is equal to $\frac{1}{2}$? How do you know?

$\frac{3}{6}$; The point for $\frac{1}{2}$ on the number line is at the tick mark for $\frac{3}{6}$.

2. a. Draw and label a point to show $\frac{1}{4}$ on the number line.

b. What fraction with a denominator of 8 is equal to $\frac{1}{4}$?

$\frac{2}{8}$

3. Grant shaded a circle to show $\frac{1}{2}$.

Grant's Circle   Your Circle

a. The circle on the right shows fourths. Shade it to show a fraction equal to $\frac{1}{2}$.

b. What fraction with a denominator of 4 is equal to $\frac{1}{2}$?

$\frac{2}{4}$

CC 31   Copyright © Pearson Education, Inc., or its affiliates. All Rights Reserved. 3

---

page CC 32

4. a. Draw and label a point to show $\frac{3}{4}$ on the number line.

b. Explain how you knew where to draw the point for $\frac{3}{4}$.

Possible answer: I divided the distance between 0 and 1 into 4 equal parts. Then I moved 3 equal parts to the right of 0.

c. What fraction with a denominator of 8 is equal to $\frac{3}{4}$?

$\frac{6}{8}$

5. Rachel shaded a circle to show $\frac{4}{6}$.

a. Shade the circle below to show a fraction equal to $\frac{4}{6}$.

b. What fraction of your circle is shaded?

$\frac{2}{3}$

6. Abby and Will each shaded a fraction of a rectangle.

Abby:
Will:

a. What fraction did Abby shade?

$\frac{2}{4}$

b. What fraction did Will shade?

$\frac{4}{8}$

c. Are the two fractions equal? How do you know?

Yes. The same amount of each rectangle is shaded.

CC 32   Copyright © Pearson Education, Inc., or its affiliates. All Rights Reserved. 3

T8

page CC 33

Name _____

Common Core Standards Practice

3.NF.A.3b Explain equivalence of fractions in special cases, and compare fractions by reasoning about their size. Recognize and generate simple equivalent fractions, e.g., $\frac{1}{2} = \frac{2}{4}$, $\frac{4}{6} = \frac{2}{3}$. Explain why the fractions are equivalent, e.g., by using a visual fraction model.

1. Which model shows a fraction equivalent to $\frac{3}{6}$?

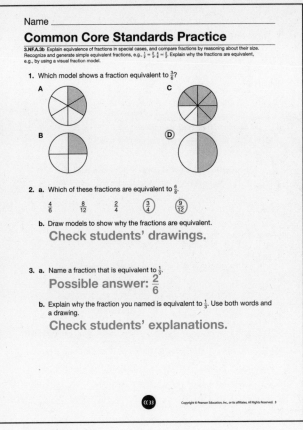

2. a. Which of these fractions are equivalent to $\frac{6}{8}$?

$\frac{4}{6}$ $\frac{8}{12}$ $\frac{2}{4}$ $\left(\frac{3}{4}\right)$ $\left(\frac{9}{12}\right)$

b. Draw models to show why the fractions are equivalent.

Check students' drawings.

3. a. Name a fraction that is equivalent to $\frac{1}{3}$.

Possible answer: $\frac{2}{6}$

b. Explain why the fraction you named is equivalent to $\frac{1}{3}$. Use both words and a drawing.

Check students' explanations.

CC 33   Copyright © Pearson Education, Inc., or its affiliates. All Rights Reserved. 3

page CC 34

4. a. Which of these fractions are equivalent to $\frac{2}{8}$?

$\left(\frac{3}{12}\right)$ $\frac{4}{12}$ $\left(\frac{1}{4}\right)$ $\frac{2}{4}$ $\frac{3}{6}$

b. Draw models to show why the fractions are equivalent.

Check students' drawings.

5. a. Which of these fractions are equivalent to $\frac{1}{2}$?

$\frac{4}{6}$ $\left(\frac{3}{6}\right)$ $\frac{2}{3}$ $\left(\frac{2}{4}\right)$ $\left(\frac{4}{8}\right)$

b. Use the number line to show why the fractions are equivalent.

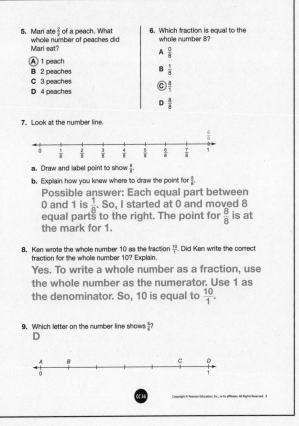

6. a. Name a fraction that is equivalent to $\frac{4}{6}$.

Possible answer: $\frac{2}{3}$

b. Explain why the fraction you named is equivalent to $\frac{4}{6}$. Use both words and a drawing.

Check students' explanations.

7. Miguel ate $\frac{2}{4}$ of an apple. April ate an equivalent fraction of an apple. Which could be the fraction that April ate?

A $\frac{2}{8}$

B $\frac{1}{3}$

Ⓒ $\frac{3}{6}$

D $\frac{3}{4}$

CC 34   Copyright © Pearson Education, Inc., or its affiliates. All Rights Reserved. 3

page CC 35

Name _____

Common Core Standards Practice

3.NF.A.3c Explain equivalence of fractions in special cases, and compare fractions by reasoning about their size. Express whole numbers as fractions, and recognize fractions that are equivalent to whole numbers.

1. Which fraction is equal to 5?

A $\frac{1}{5}$

B $\frac{2}{5}$

Ⓒ $\frac{5}{1}$

D $\frac{5}{5}$

2. Explain how to write the whole number 4 as a fraction.

Use the whole number as the numerator. Use 1 as the denominator. The whole number 4 is equal to the fraction $\frac{4}{1}$.

3. Look at the number line.

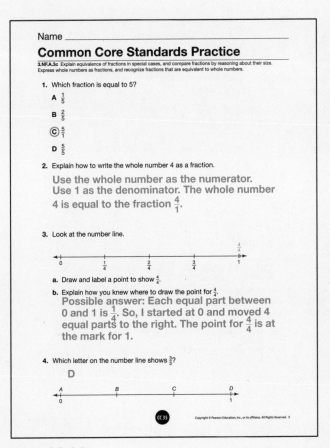

a. Draw and label a point to show $\frac{4}{4}$.

b. Explain how you knew where to draw the point for $\frac{4}{4}$.

Possible answer: Each equal part between 0 and 1 is $\frac{1}{4}$. So, I started at 0 and moved 4 equal parts to the right. The point for $\frac{4}{4}$ is at the mark for 1.

4. Which letter on the number line shows $\frac{3}{3}$?

D

CC 35   Copyright © Pearson Education, Inc., or its affiliates. All Rights Reserved. 3

page CC 36

5. Mari ate $\frac{2}{2}$ of a peach. What whole number of peaches did Mari eat?

Ⓐ 1 peach

B 2 peaches

C 3 peaches

D 4 peaches

6. Which fraction is equal to the whole number 8?

A $\frac{0}{8}$

B $\frac{1}{8}$

Ⓒ $\frac{8}{1}$

D $\frac{8}{8}$

7. Look at the number line.

a. Draw and label point to show $\frac{8}{8}$.

b. Explain how you knew where to draw the point for $\frac{8}{8}$.

Possible answer: Each equal part between 0 and 1 is $\frac{1}{8}$. So, I started at 0 and moved 8 equal parts to the right. The point for $\frac{8}{8}$ is at the mark for 1.

8. Ken wrote the whole number 10 as the fraction $\frac{10}{1}$. Did Ken write the correct fraction for the whole number 10? Explain.

Yes. To write a whole number as a fraction, use the whole number as the numerator. Use 1 as the denominator. So, 10 is equal to $\frac{10}{1}$.

9. Which letter on the number line shows $\frac{6}{6}$?

D

CC 36   Copyright © Pearson Education, Inc., or its affiliates. All Rights Reserved. 3

T9

Page CC 37

Common Core Standards Practice

3.NF.A.3d Explain equivalence of fractions in special cases, and compare fractions by reasoning about their size. Compare two fractions with the same numerator or the same denominator by reasoning about their size. Recognize that comparisons are valid only when the two fractions refer to the same whole. Record the results of comparisons with the symbols >, =, or <, and justify the conclusions, e.g., by using a visual fraction model.

1. a. Which fraction is greater, $\frac{2}{6}$ or $\frac{4}{6}$?

$$\frac{4}{6}$$

b. Explain how you know which fraction is greater.

Possible answer: $\frac{2}{6}$ is 2 parts of size $\frac{1}{6}$. $\frac{4}{6}$ is 4 parts of size $\frac{1}{6}$. 4 parts are greater than 2 parts of the same size.

2. Sadie ate $\frac{2}{8}$ of a small pizza. Josef ate $\frac{2}{8}$ of a large pizza. Did Sadie and Josef eat the same amount of pizza? Explain.

No. Josef's pizza is larger. So, $\frac{2}{8}$ of Josef's pizza is a larger amount than $\frac{2}{8}$ of Sadie's pizza.

3. a. Which fraction is greater, $\frac{5}{8}$ or $\frac{5}{6}$?

$$\frac{5}{6}$$

b. Explain how you know which fraction is greater.

Possible answer: $\frac{5}{8}$ is 5 parts of size $\frac{1}{8}$. $\frac{5}{6}$ is 5 parts of size $\frac{1}{6}$. Parts of size $\frac{1}{6}$ are larger than parts of size $\frac{1}{8}$, so $\frac{5}{6}$ is greater than $\frac{5}{8}$.

4. Place the fractions below in the appropriate place.

Less than $\frac{1}{2}$	Equal to $\frac{1}{2}$	Greater than $\frac{1}{2}$
$\frac{3}{8}$ $\frac{2}{8}$	$\frac{2}{4}$	$\frac{4}{6}$ $\frac{7}{8}$
$\frac{1}{3}$ $\frac{5}{12}$	$\frac{3}{6}$	$\frac{5}{8}$ $\frac{6}{10}$

$\frac{3}{8}$ $\frac{4}{6}$ $\frac{2}{4}$ $\frac{5}{8}$ $\frac{1}{3}$

$\frac{5}{12}$ $\frac{2}{8}$ $\frac{6}{10}$ $\frac{3}{6}$ $\frac{7}{8}$

page CC 37

Page CC 38

5. Which fraction is less than $\frac{2}{6}$?

(A) $\frac{2}{8}$

B $\frac{2}{4}$

C $\frac{3}{6}$

D $\frac{5}{6}$

6. Circle the smaller fraction.

$\frac{6}{8}$ $\left(\frac{3}{8}\right)$

7. Ben and Theo each have an orange. The oranges are the same size. Ben eats $\frac{2}{3}$ of his orange. Theo eats $\frac{2}{4}$ of his orange.

a. Did Ben or Theo eat a larger fraction of the orange?

Ben

b. Draw models of each fraction to show that your answer is correct.

Check students' drawings.

8. a. Which fraction is larger, $\frac{1}{4}$ or $\frac{3}{4}$?

$$\frac{3}{4}$$

b. Use the number line to show that your answer is correct.

0    $\frac{1}{4}$ $\frac{2}{4}$ $\frac{3}{4}$ 1

9. Alonso painted $\frac{1}{2}$ of a large wall. Adele painted $\frac{1}{2}$ of a small wall. Do you think they used the same amount of paint? Explain.

Sample answer: No; The walls are different sizes. So, $\frac{1}{2}$ of the large wall is a greater amount than $\frac{1}{2}$ of the small wall. A greater amount of wall probably needs a greater amount of paint.

page CC 38

Page CC 39

Common Core Standards Practice

3.MD.A.1 Tell and write time to the nearest minute and measure time intervals in minutes. Solve word problems involving addition and subtraction of time intervals in minutes, e.g., by representing the problem on a number line diagram.

1. Write the time shown on the clock.

2 : 14

2. Alex leaves for school every day at 8:20. Show this time on the clock below.

3. After school each day, Devin spends 25 minutes on his math homework and 15 minutes on his language arts homework. How many minutes does Devin spend doing his math and language arts homework?

40 minutes

4. Laura goes to lunch at the time shown on the clock. At what time does she go to lunch?

11 : 55

5. Lily and her parents drove to her grandmother's house. They arrived at her grandmother's house at 9:40 a.m. The drive took 45 minutes. At what time did Lily and her parents leave their house?

a. Model this problem on the number line.

Check students' work.

b. Tell what time Lily and her parents left their house.

8:55 A.M.

page CC 39

Page CC 40

6. Tristan's math class starts at 1:37. Draw hands on the clock to show 1:37.

7. A play ended at 7:30. It began 1 hour and 10 minutes earlier. At what time did the play begin?

6 : 20

8. What time does the clock show?

5 : 22

9. After school, Marta and her sister play one game for 45 minutes. Then they play another game for 30 minutes. For how long did Marta and her sister play games?

75 minutes

10. Julia got on the bus at 2:20 P.M. She got off the bus 50 minutes later. At what time did she get off the bus?

a. Model this problem on the number line.

Check students' work.

b. Tell what time Julie got off the bus.

3:10 P.M.

page CC 40

Common Core Standards Practice

3.MD.A.2 Measure and estimate liquid volumes and masses of objects using standard units of grams (g), kilograms (kg), and liters (l). Add, subtract, multiply, or divide to solve one-step word problems involving masses or volumes that are given in the same units, e.g., by using drawings (such as a beaker with a measurement scale) to represent the problem.

1. Which is the best estimate of the capacity of the pitcher?

(A) 1 liter
B 5 liters
C 10 liters
D 100 liters

2. Mr. Roberts went to the farmer's market on Wednesday and bought 450 grams of ground beef and 600 grams of ground pork. How much meat did Mr. Robert buy on Wednesday?

A 250 grams
B 510 grams
(C) 1,050 grams
D 1,150 grams

3. Circle the best estimate for the mass of the pillow.

(1 kg) 10 kg 100 kg

4. A bathtub holds 150 liters of water. A sink holds 12 liters of water. How many more liters of water does the bathtub hold than the sink?

138 liters

5. Ryan has 2 apples. One has a mass of 130 grams. The other has a mass of 124 grams. What is the combined mass of the two apples?

254 grams

6. How many liters of water are in the bucket?

12 L
10 L
8 L
6 L
4 L
2 L

4 liters

page CC 41

---

7. A bag of food has a mass of 20 kilograms. A worker at a zoo uses all of the food in the bag to feed 10 animals. She gives each animal an equal share of the food. How many kilograms of food does each animal get?

(A) 2 kilograms
B 10 kilograms
C 30 kilograms
D 200 kilograms

8. Circle the best estimate for the mass of the bowling ball.

400 kg   40 kg   (4 kg)

9. What is the mass of the tomatoes on the scale?

300 grams

10. In science class, Ashton put 150 milliliters of oil in the beaker. Then he put 50 milliliters of vinegar into the same beaker.

a. On the beaker below, show the amount of oil and vinegar Ashton put in the beaker.

500 ml
400 ml
300 ml
200 ml
100 ml

b. How many milliliters of liquid did Ashton put in the beaker?

200 milliliters

11. Blanca bought 9 bottles of juice for a party. Each bottle holds 2 liters of juice. How many liters of juice did Blanca buy?

a. What operation do you need to use to solve the problem? Explain why?

multiplication. Check students' explanations.

b. How many liters of juice did Blanca buy?

18 liters

page CC 42

Common Core Standards Practice

3.MD.B.3 Draw a scaled picture graph and a scaled bar graph to represent a data set with several categories. Solve one- and two-step "how many more" and "how many less" problems using information presented in scaled bar graphs.

1. Use the information in the tally chart to complete the picture graph.

Favorite Sports of Third Graders

Sport	Tally
Baseball	|||||	
Football	||||| |||
Soccer	||||| ||||| ||

Favorite Sports of Third Graders

Baseball	◯ ◯ ◯
Football	◯ ◯ ◯ ◯
Soccer	◯ ◯ ◯ ◯ ◯ ◯
Key: ◯ stands for 2 students	

How many more students picked soccer as their favorite sport than baseball? Tell how you know.

6 more students; check students' explanations

The picture graph below shows how the third-grade students at a school get to school each day. Use the picture graph for questions 2 and 3.

Ways to Get to School

Bus	✿ ✿ ✿ ✿ ✿
Bike	✿
Walk	✿ ✿
Car	✿ ✿ ✿ ✿
Key: ✿ stands for 6 students	

2. How many fewer students walk to school than ride in a car?

12 students

3. How many more students take the bus to school than walk or bike?

18 students

page CC 43

---

4. The table shows the number of laps that 4 students swam last week. Use the information in the table to complete the bar graph.

Name	Laps
Molly	50
Fred	40
Jessica	45
Mateo	30

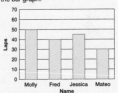

The bar graph below shows the number of some of the animals at a zoo. Use the bar graph for questions 5 and 6.

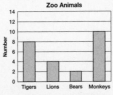

5. How many fewer bears than tigers are at the zoo?

6 fewer

6. Lions and tigers are large cats. How many more large cats than monkeys are at the zoo?

2 more

page CC 44

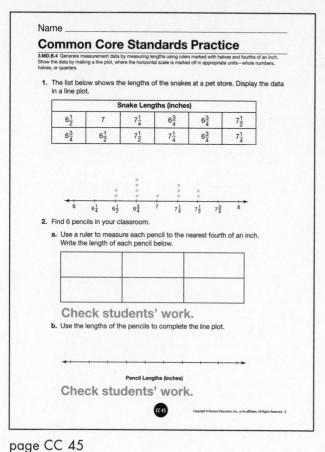

Name

Common Core Standards Practice

3.MD.B.4 Generate measurement data by measuring lengths using rulers marked with halves and fourths of an inch. Show the data by making a line plot, where the horizontal scale is marked off in appropriate units—whole numbers, halves, or quarters.

1. The list below shows the lengths of the snakes at a pet store. Display the data in a line plot.

Snake Lengths (inches)					
$6\frac{1}{2}$	7	$7\frac{1}{4}$	$6\frac{3}{4}$	$6\frac{3}{4}$	$7\frac{1}{2}$
$6\frac{3}{4}$	$6\frac{1}{2}$	$7\frac{1}{2}$	$7\frac{1}{4}$	$6\frac{3}{4}$	$7\frac{1}{4}$

2. Find 6 pencils in your classroom.

   a. Use a ruler to measure each pencil to the nearest fourth of an inch. Write the length of each pencil below.

   Check students' work.

   b. Use the lengths of the pencils to complete the line plot.

   Pencil Lengths (inches)

   Check students' work.

page CC 45

---

3. The list below shows the lengths of Aaron's toy cars. Use the information to complete the line plot.

Car Lengths (inches)				
1	$1\frac{3}{4}$	2	$1\frac{1}{2}$	2
1	$1\frac{1}{2}$	2	2	1

Car Lengths (inches)

4. Find 6 crayons in your classroom.

   a. Use a ruler to measure each crayon to the nearest fourth of an inch. Write the length of each crayon below.

   Check students' work.

   b. Use the lengths of the crayons to complete the line plot.

   Crayon Lengths (inches)

   Check students' work.

page CC 46

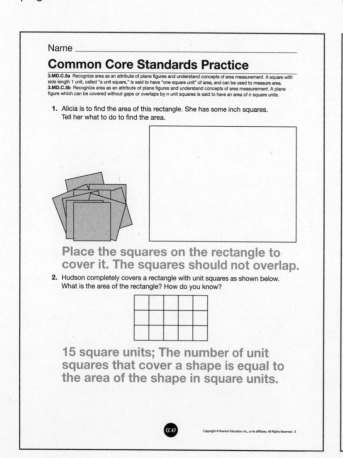

Name

Common Core Standards Practice

3.MD.C.5a Recognize area as an attribute of plane figures and understand concepts of area measurement. A square with side length 1 unit, called "a unit square," is said to have "one square unit" of area, and can be used to measure area.
3.MD.C.5b Recognize area as an attribute of plane figures and understand concepts of area measurement. A plane figure which can be covered without gaps or overlaps by n unit squares is said to have an area of n square units.

1. Alicia is to find the area of this rectangle. She has some inch squares. Tell her what to do to find the area.

   Place the squares on the rectangle to cover it. The squares should not overlap.

2. Hudson completely covers a rectangle with unit squares as shown below. What is the area of the rectangle? How do you know?

   15 square units; The number of unit squares that cover a shape is equal to the area of the shape in square units.

page CC 47

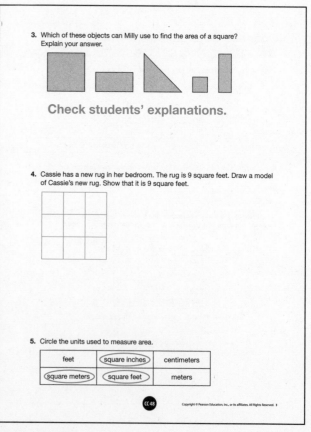

3. Which of these objects can Milly use to find the area of a square? Explain your answer.

   Check students' explanations.

4. Cassie has a new rug in her bedroom. The rug is 9 square feet. Draw a model of Cassie's new rug. Show that it is 9 square feet.

5. Circle the units used to measure area.

feet	square inches	centimeters
square meters	square feet	meters

page CC 48

page CC 49

Name _____

Common Core Standards Practice

3.MD.C.6 Measure areas by counting unit squares (square cm, square m, square in, square ft, and improvised units).

1. What is the area of the rectangle below?

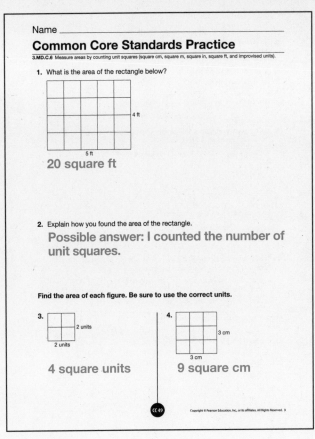

4 ft

5 ft

20 square ft

2. Explain how you found the area of the rectangle.

Possible answer: I counted the number of unit squares.

Find the area of each figure. Be sure to use the correct units.

3.

2 units

2 units

4 square units

4.

3 cm

3 cm

9 square cm

page CC 49

---

page CC 50

Find the area of each figure. Be sure to use the correct units.

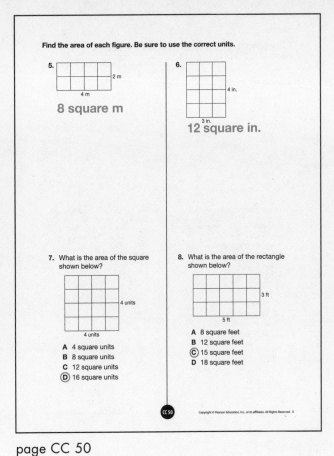

5.

2 m

4 m

8 square m

6.

4 in.

3 in.

12 square in.

7. What is the area of the square shown below?

4 units

4 units

A 4 square units
B 8 square units
C 12 square units
D 16 square units ✓

8. What is the area of the rectangle shown below?

3 ft

5 ft

A 8 square feet
B 12 square feet
C 15 square feet ✓
D 18 square feet

page CC 50

---

page CC 51

Name _____

Common Core Standards Practice

3.MD.C.7a Relate area to the operations of multiplication and addition. Find the area of a rectangle with whole-number side lengths by tiling it, and show that the area is the same as would be found by multiplying the side lengths.

Look at the rectangle on the grid.

1. What is the area of the rectangle above? Tell how you know.

30 square cm; check students' explanations.

2. What is the length of the rectangle above? Tell how you determined the length.

6 centimeters. I counted the number of squares that the length covers.

3. What is the height of the rectangle above? Tell how you determined the height.

5 centimeters. I counted the number of squares that the height covers.

4. How does the product of the length and height relate to the number of squares that the rectangle covers?

They are the same. The product of the length and height is 30 and the number of squares covering the rectangle is 30.

page CC 51

---

page CC 52

5. Look at the rectangle below.

2 ft

4 ft

a. How many squares cover the rectangle?

8 squares

b. Multiply the length and the width of the rectangle. What answer do you get?

8 square units

c. What do you notice about the answers in part a and part b? What does that tell you about finding the area?

They are the same. Check students' work. Sample answer: You can find the area of a rectangle by counting the squares or multiplying the length and width.

6. a. Give two different ways to find the area of the square.

One way is to count unit squares. Another way is to multiply the length and width.

3 in.

3 in.

b. Use both ways to find the area of the square.

First way: Area = **9 square in.**

Second way: Area = **9 square in.**

c. Do you get the same answer? Why?

Yes. There are 3 rows of 3 unit squares, so finding 3 × 3 gives the correct number of unit squares.

page CC 52

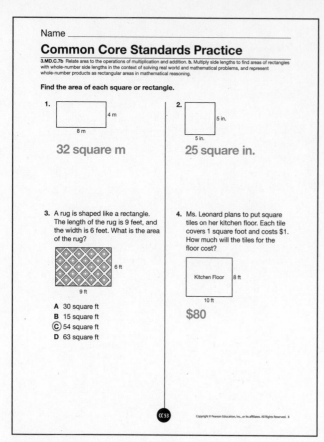

page CC 53

Name _____

Common Core Standards Practice

3.MD.C.7b Relate area to the operations of multiplication and addition. b. Multiply side lengths to find areas of rectangles with whole-number side lengths in the context of solving real world and mathematical problems, and represent whole-number products as rectangular areas in mathematical reasoning.

Find the area of each square or rectangle.

1.
4 m
8 m

32 square m

2.
5 in.
5 in.

25 square in.

3. A rug is shaped like a rectangle. The length of the rug is 9 feet, and the width is 6 feet. What is the area of the rug?

6 ft
9 ft

A 30 square ft
B 15 square ft
Ⓒ 54 square ft
D 63 square ft

4. Ms. Leonard plans to put square tiles on her kitchen floor. Each tile covers 1 square foot and costs $1. How much will the tiles for the floor cost?

Kitchen Floor 8 ft
10 ft

$80

CC 53   Copyright © Pearson Education, Inc., or its affiliates. All Rights Reserved. 3

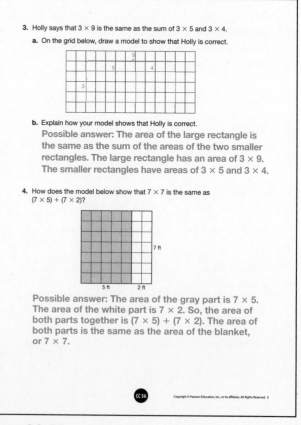

page CC 54

5. Troy wants to make a pen for his rabbits. The pen will be a rectangle with an area of 24 square meters. Answer Yes or No if the length and width could be the dimensions of Troy's rabbit pen.

A length: 2 m, width: 6 m   YES   (NO)
B length: 3 m, width: 8 m   (YES)   NO
C length: 5 m, width: 5 m   YES   (NO)
D length: 4 m, width: 6 m   (YES)   NO

6. Izzie is planting a garden. Her garden is shaped like a rectangle. The length is 7 feet, and the width is 3 feet.

a. Draw a picture of Izzie's garden. Label the length and width.

3 ft
7 ft

b. What is the area of Izzie's garden?

Area = **21 square ft**

7. The drawing shows the lid of a box. Lorrie is gluing square tiles to the lid. Each tile has an area of 1 square centimeter.

a. How many tiles will Lorrie need to completely cover the lid?

25 tiles

5 cm
5 cm

b. Explain how you found your answer.

Possible answer: I multiplied the length and width to find the area of the lid. The area is 25 square cm. Lorrie needs 1 tile for each square cm, so she needs 25 tiles.

CC 54   Copyright © Pearson Education, Inc., or its affiliates. All Rights Reserved. 3

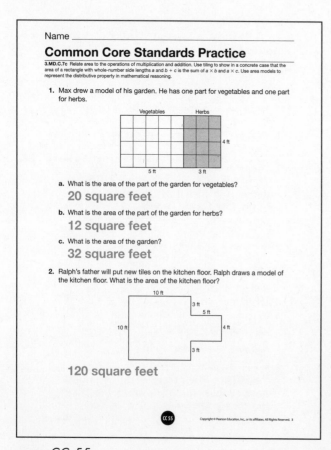

page CC 55

Name _____

Common Core Standards Practice

3.MD.C.7c Relate area to the operations of multiplication and addition. Use tiling to show in a concrete case that the area of a rectangle with whole-number side lengths a and b + c is the sum of a × b and a × c. Use area models to represent the distributive property in mathematical reasoning.

1. Max drew a model of his garden. He has one part for vegetables and one part for herbs.

Vegetables   Herbs
4 ft
5 ft   3 ft

a. What is the area of the part of the garden for vegetables?
20 square feet

b. What is the area of the part of the garden for herbs?
12 square feet

c. What is the area of the garden?
32 square feet

2. Ralph's father will put new tiles on the kitchen floor. Ralph draws a model of the kitchen floor. What is the area of the kitchen floor?

10 ft
3 ft
5 ft
10 ft   4 ft
3 ft

120 square feet

CC 55   Copyright © Pearson Education, Inc., or its affiliates. All Rights Reserved. 3

---

page CC 56

3. Holly says that 3 × 9 is the same as the sum of 3 × 5 and 3 × 4.

a. On the grid below, draw a model to show that Holly is correct.

9
5   4
3

b. Explain how your model shows that Holly is correct.

Possible answer: The area of the large rectangle is the same as the sum of the areas of the two smaller rectangles. The large rectangle has an area of 3 × 9. The smaller rectangles have areas of 3 × 5 and 3 × 4.

4. How does the model below show that 7 × 7 is the same as (7 × 5) + (7 × 2)?

7 ft
5 ft   2 ft

Possible answer: The area of the gray part is 7 × 5. The area of the white part is 7 × 2. So, the area of both parts together is (7 × 5) + (7 × 2). The area of both parts is the same as the area of the blanket, or 7 × 7.

CC 56   Copyright © Pearson Education, Inc., or its affiliates. All Rights Reserved. 3

T14

Common Core Standards Practice

3.MD.C.7d Relate area to the operations of multiplication and addition. Recognize area as additive. Find areas of rectilinear figures by decomposing them into non-overlapping rectangles and adding the areas of the non-overlapping parts, applying this technique to solve real world problems.

1. Linda's bedroom floor has side lengths of 12 feet and 9 feet. She drew a picture of the floor, and then broke it apart into two smaller rectangles.

   a. What is the area of each smaller rectangle?

   90 square ft and 18 square ft

   b. What is the total area of the floor? How do you know?

   108 square ft; The area of the floor is equal to the sum of the areas of the smaller rectangles. So, the area of the floor is 90 + 18 = 108 square ft.

2. Curt made a bookmark in the shape of a rectangle. The bookmark has a length of 15 centimeters and a width of 5 centimeters.

   a. Break apart the bookmark into two smaller rectangles to make it easier to find the area. **Possible answer:**

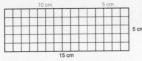

   b. What is the area of the bookmark? Show your work.

   75 square cm

page CC 57

---

3. A driveway has the shape of a rectangle. It is 16 meters long and 4 meters wide.

   a. Break apart the driveway into two smaller rectangles to make it easier to find the area. **Possible answer:**

   b. What is the area of the driveway? Show your work.

   64 square m

   c. Explain how breaking apart the driveway made it easier to find the area.

   Possible answer: The areas of the smaller rectangles are the same as 4 × 10 and 4 × 6. These products are easier to find than 4 × 16.

4. A mirror has the shape of a rectangle. It is 13 inches long and 6 inches wide. What is the area of the mirror? Show your work.

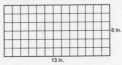

   Check students' work. 78 square in.

page CC 58

Common Core Standards Practice

3.MD.D.8 Solve real world and mathematical problems involving perimeters of polygons, including finding the perimeter given the side lengths, finding an unknown side length, and exhibiting rectangles with the same perimeter and different areas or with the same area and different perimeters.

1. Harry's father is building a tree house. The model below represents the floor. What will be the perimeter of the floor?

Perimeter = **36 in.**

2. Ama is making a banner. The model below represents her banner. She will put gold cord around the banner. How many centimeters of gold cord will she use?

Perimeter = **9 cm**

3. The perimeter of the triangle is 9 centimeters. What is the missing side length?

3 cm

4. The perimeter of the figure is 20 inches. What is the missing side length?

4 in.

5. The drawing shows the yard of the Lang family. What is the perimeter of the yard?

71 m; Check students' work.

page CC 59

---

6. Look at the rectangle shown below.

   a. What are the perimeter and area of the rectangle?

   Perimeter = **14 m**   Area = **10 square m**

   b. On the grid, draw a rectangle that has the same perimeter, but a different area.

   Possible answers include 6 m by 1 m and 4 m by 3 m.

   c. What is the area of the rectangle you drew?

   Check students' work.

7. A farmer needs to build a new animal corral in the shape of a rectangle. The pen needs to have an area of 72 square meters. He will need to buy fencing to go around the corral.

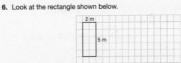

   a. What could be the dimensions of the corral? Draw models of two different rectangles with an area of 72 square meters. Label the length and width of each model.

   Possible answers: 8 m by 9 m, 4 m by 18 m, and 12 m by 6 m.

   b. Which of your models will require more fencing? Tell how you know.

   Check students' work. The 8 m by 9 m corral requires the least fencing (34 m); the 4 m by 18 m corral requires the most fencing (44 m).

page CC 60

Page CC 61

Common Core Standards Practice

3.G.A.1 Understand that shapes in different categories (e.g., rhombuses, rectangles, and others) may share attributes (e.g., having four sides), and that the shared attributes can define a larger category (e.g., quadrilaterals). Recognize rhombuses, rectangles, and squares as examples of quadrilaterals, and draw examples of quadrilaterals that do not belong to any of these subcategories.

1. What are two ways these shapes are alike?

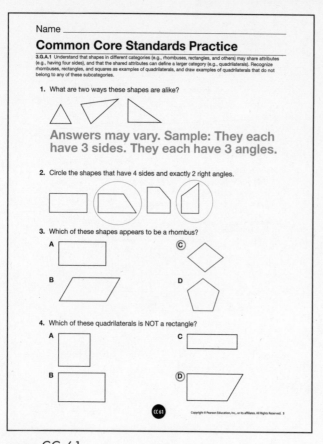

Answers may vary. Sample: They each have 3 sides. They each have 3 angles.

2. Circle the shapes that have 4 sides and exactly 2 right angles.

3. Which of these shapes appears to be a rhombus?

A

B

Ⓒ

D

4. Which of these quadrilaterals is NOT a rectangle?

A

B

C

Ⓓ

CC 61
Copyright © Pearson Education, Inc., or its affiliates. All Rights Reserved. 3

page CC 61

Page CC 62

5. a. Draw a quadrilateral that is not a rhombus, a square, or a rectangle.

Check students' drawings.

b. Explain how you know that your quadrilateral is not a rhombus, a square, or a rectangle.

Answers may vary. Sample: It does not have 4 right angles, so it is not a square or a rectangle. It does not have 4 sides of the same length, so it is not a rhombus.

6. What is one way these shapes are alike?

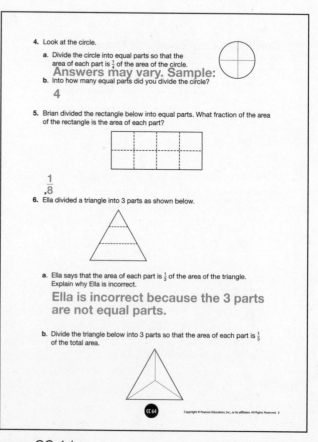

Answers may vary. Sample: They each have 5 sides.

7. a. Circle the quadrilateral that appears to be a square.

b. Explain how you know that the quadrilateral you picked is a square.

It appears to have 4 right angles. Its sides appear to have the same length.

CC 62
Copyright © Pearson Education, Inc., or its affiliates. All Rights Reserved. 3

page CC 62

Page CC 63

Common Core Standards Practice

3.G.A.2 Partition shapes into parts with equal areas. Express the area of each part as a unit fraction of the whole.

1. The rectangle is divided into 4 equal parts. What fraction of the area of the rectangle is the area of each part?

Ⓐ $\frac{1}{4}$ C $\frac{1}{2}$

B $\frac{1}{3}$ D $\frac{3}{4}$

2. Look at the hexagon.

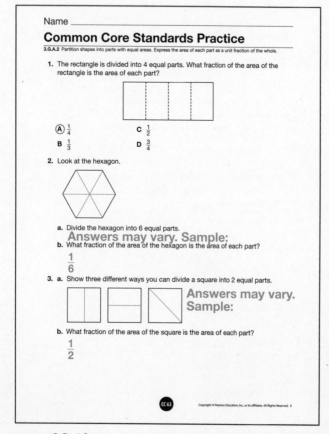

a. Divide the hexagon into 6 equal parts.

Answers may vary. Sample:

b. What fraction of the area of the hexagon is the area of each part?

$\frac{1}{6}$

3. a. Show three different ways you can divide a square into 2 equal parts.

Answers may vary. Sample:

b. What fraction of the area of the square is the area of each part?

$\frac{1}{2}$

CC 63
Copyright © Pearson Education, Inc., or its affiliates. All Rights Reserved. 3

page CC 63

Page CC 64

4. Look at the circle.

a. Divide the circle into equal parts so that the area of each part is $\frac{1}{4}$ of the area of the circle.

Answers may vary. Sample:

b. Into how many equal parts did you divide the circle?

4

5. Brian divided the rectangle below into equal parts. What fraction of the area of the rectangle is the area of each part?

$\frac{1}{8}$

6. Ella divided a triangle into 3 parts as shown below.

a. Ella says that the area of each part is $\frac{1}{3}$ of the area of the triangle. Explain why Ella is incorrect.

Ella is incorrect because the 3 parts are not equal parts.

b. Divide the triangle below into 3 parts so that the area of each part is $\frac{1}{3}$ of the total area.

CC 64
Copyright © Pearson Education, Inc., or its affiliates. All Rights Reserved. 3

page CC 64

Name _____

Practice End-of-Year Assessment

1. The bar graph shows the favorite pets of the third grade.

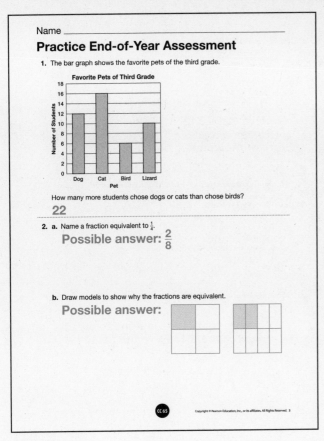

Favorite Pets of Third Grade

How many more students chose dogs or cats than chose birds?

22

2. a. Name a fraction equivalent to $\frac{1}{4}$.

Possible answer: $\frac{2}{8}$

b. Draw models to show why the fractions are equivalent.

Possible answer:

page CC 65

---

3. Sara buys 6 pencils with a $20 bill. Each pencil costs $2.

a. How much change should Sara receive?

$8

b. Explain how you found your answer.

Possible answer: First, I multiplied 6 by $2 to find the total cost of the pencils. Then I subtracted $12 from $20 to find the amount of change.

4. Which of these numbers round to 1,780 when rounded to the nearest ten? Circle all that apply.

(1,784)   1,874   (1,775)

1,708   (1,779)   1,799

5. There are 3 rows of cans. Each row has 4 cans.

a. Draw an array to show how many cans there are in all.

Check students' arrays.

b. How many cans are there in all?

12

page CC 66

---

6. Divide the number line into three equal parts. Then draw and label a point to show $\frac{1}{3}$.

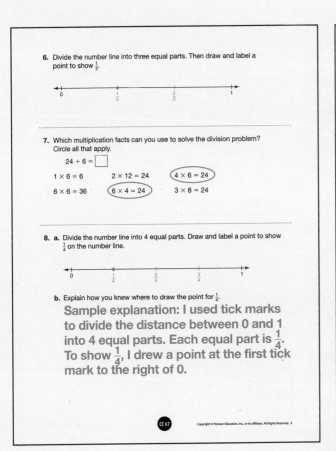

7. Which multiplication facts can you use to solve the division problem? Circle all that apply.

$24 \div 6 = \boxed{}$

$1 \times 6 = 6$ $2 \times 12 = 24$ ($4 \times 6 = 24$)

$6 \times 6 = 36$ ($6 \times 4 = 24$) $3 \times 8 = 24$

8. a. Divide the number line into 4 equal parts. Draw and label a point to show $\frac{1}{4}$ on the number line.

b. Explain how you knew where to draw the point for $\frac{1}{4}$.

Sample explanation: I used tick marks to divide the distance between 0 and 1 into 4 equal parts. Each equal part is $\frac{1}{4}$. To show $\frac{1}{4}$, I drew a point at the first tick mark to the right of 0.

page CC 67

---

9. Compare the fractions. Write >, =, or <.

$\frac{1}{5} > \frac{1}{9}$

Explain how you know which fraction is greater. Draw a model to support your explanation.

Check students' explanations. They should say that 1 fifth of a circle is larger than 1 ninth of a circle.

10. For which of these equations is 3 the missing factor? Circle all that apply.

($6 \times \boxed{} = 18$) $\boxed{} \times 4 = 16$ $8 \times \boxed{} = 16$

($7 \times \boxed{} = 21$)   ($\boxed{} \times 9 = 27$) $3 \times \boxed{} = 12$

11. Look at the column for 4 in the multiplication table. What pattern do you see?

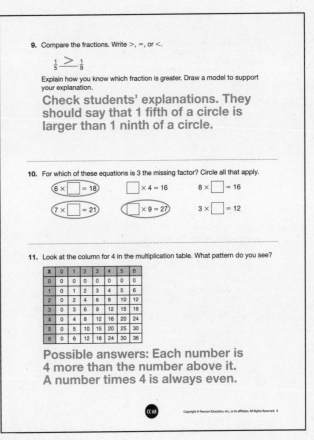

X	0	1	2	3	4	5	6
0	0	0	0	0	0	0	0
1	0	1	2	3	4	5	6
2	0	2	4	6	8	10	12
3	0	3	6	9	12	15	18
4	0	4	8	12	16	20	24
5	0	5	10	15	20	25	30
6	0	6	12	18	24	30	36

Possible answers: Each number is 4 more than the number above it. A number times 4 is always even.

page CC 68

12. Leo needs 4 pieces of tape, each 5 inches long.

    a. Write an equation to show how much tape Leo needs in all. Use the letter *t* to stand for the missing number.

Possible answer: 4 × 5 = *t*

    b. How many inches of tape does Leo need in all?

20 inches

---

13. Baseball practice ended at 4:10. It began 30 minutes earlier. Which shows when baseball practice began?

(A) 3:40
B 3:10
C 4:40
D 3:50

---

14. Tell how to find 4 × 9 by breaking apart 9 into 5 + 4. You can use words or models.

(4 × 5) + (4 × 4) = 20 + 16 = 36

page CC 69

---

15. A cook makes 3 pots of soup. Each pot holds 8 liters of soup. How many liters of soup did the cook make in all?

24 liters

---

16. Look at the numbers in the table. What pattern do you see?

4	9	14	19	24

Possible answer: Each number is 5 more than the number before it.

---

17. There are 28 people going on a boat ride. Each boat can hold 4 people.

    a. Write an equation to show how many boats they will need. Use the letter *b* to stand for the missing number.

Possible answer: 28 ÷ 4 = *b*

    b. How many boats will they need?

7 boats

---

18. What is the area of the rectangle? Be sure to use the correct units.

20 square centimeters

page CC 70

---

19. A fish has a mass of 26 kilograms. The mass of a turtle is 8 kilograms less than the mass of the fish. What is the mass of the turtle?

18 kilograms

---

20. a. What is the missing number in the equation?

9 × 8 = 8 × 9

    b. Explain how you know.

Possible answer: You can multiply numbers in any order. The product will stay the same. So, 9 × 8 is the same as 8 × 9.

---

21. a. Write a word problem that matches 12 ÷ 4.

Possible answer: Donna has 12 stickers. She shares the stickers equally among 4 friends. How many stickers will each friend get?

    b. Explain why your problem matches 12 ÷ 4.

Possible answer: 12 ÷ 4 gives the number of stickers in each share when 12 stickers are divided into 4 equal shares.

page CC 71

---

22. A third grade class is growing bean plants. The list below shows the heights of the plants. Use the information to complete the line plot.

Plant Heights (inches)

$7\frac{1}{2}$	6	$6\frac{1}{4}$	7	$6\frac{3}{4}$
$6\frac{1}{4}$	7	$7\frac{1}{2}$	7	$6\frac{3}{4}$

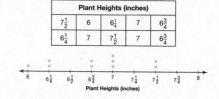

Plant Heights (inches)

---

23. For which of these equations is the missing value equal to 7? Circle all that apply.

 63 ÷ 9 = ☐   56 ÷ ☐ = 7   27 ÷ ☐ = 3

54 ÷ 6 = ☐   35 ÷ 5 = ☐   49 ÷ ☐ = 7

---

24. Write the time shown on the clock.

    _8_ . _07_

page CC 72

T18

25. a. Divide the figure into 8 equal parts. Then shade one of the parts.

Possible answer:

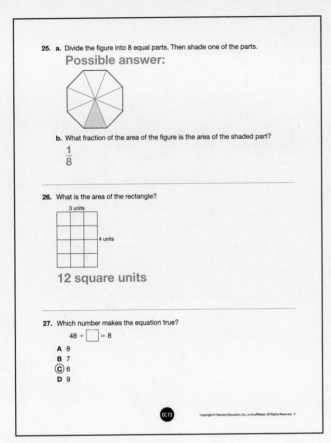

b. What fraction of the area of the figure is the area of the shaded part?

$\frac{1}{8}$

---

26. What is the area of the rectangle?

3 units

4 units

12 square units

---

27. Which number makes the equation true?

$48 \div \boxed{} = 8$

A 8
B 7
C 6
D 9

page CC 73

---

28. The perimeter of the figure is 18 feet.

3 ft
4 ft   ?
6 ft

a. What is the missing side length?   **5 feet**

b. Tell how you know.

I added the lengths of the three sides and subtracted that sum from 18.

---

29. For each equation in 29a–29d, answer Yes or No if the $\boxed{}$ = 8 makes the equation true.

a. $4 \times \boxed{} = 32$ (YES)   NO

b. $\boxed{} \times 6 = 56$ YES   (NO)

c. $5 \times \boxed{} = 40$ (YES)   NO

d. $\boxed{} \times 8 = 56$ YES   (NO)

---

30. Ms. Carr has a flowerbed in the shape of a rectangle. The flowerbed has a length of 14 feet and a width of 4 feet.

a. Break apart the flowerbed into two smaller rectangles to make it easier to find the area.

Possible answer:

10 ft   4 ft

4 ft

14 ft

b. What is the area of the flowerbed? Show your work.

56 square feet

page CC 74

---

31. How can the product of 6 and 7 help you find the product of 60 and 7?

Check students' explanations. Sample explanation: 60×7 is the product of 6 and 7 times 10.

---

32. Write a multiplication fact that can help you solve the division problem.

$36 \div 9 = \boxed{}$

$4 \times 9 = 36$ or $9 \times 4 = 36$

---

33. A door is shaped liked a rectangle. The length of the door is 7 feet, and the width is 3 feet. What is the area of the door?

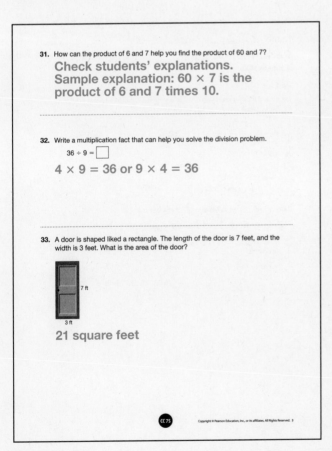

7 ft

3 ft

21 square feet

page CC 75

---

34. a. Divide the rectangle into 3 equal parts. Shade 1 of the parts.

b. What fraction of the rectangle is shaded?

$\frac{1}{3}$

---

35. Which quadrilateral does NOT have any square corners?

A

C

B

D

---

36. A flag has an area of 12 square feet. Explain what this sentence means.

Possible answer: You can completely cover the flag with 12 unit squares. Each unit square has an area of 1 square foot and a side length of 1 foot.

page CC 76

page CC 77

37. Multiply.

$$\begin{array}{r} 9 \\ \times\ 5 \\ \hline 45 \end{array}$$

38. Erin had 28 cards. She kept 8 for herself. She shared the rest equally between her 2 brothers.

   a. How many cards did each of Erin's brothers get?

   10 cards

   b. Explain how you found your answer.

   Possible answer: First, I subtracted 8 from 28 to find how many cards were left for the brothers. Then I divided 20 by 2 to find how many cards each brother got.

39. Subtract.

$$\begin{array}{r} 326 \\ -\ \ 38 \\ \hline 288 \end{array}$$

40. Mr. Padilla has 3 apples. He cuts each apple into 8 pieces. He puts 4 apple pieces into each bag.

   a. How many bags will Mr. Padilla need?

   6 bags

   b. Explain how you found your answer.

   Possible answer: First, I multiplied 3 by 8 to find how many pieces there are. Then I divided 24 by 4 to find how many bags Mr. Padilla will need.

page CC 77

---

page CC 78

Name _____

Performance Task 1
Raising Funds

Part A

The students in Ms. Jansen's third grade class are having a school bake sale. They want to raise $500 for a fieldtrip.

Ms. Jansen asked her students' families to volunteer to bring in brownies, cookies, or large cupcakes for the sale.

From the volunteer sign-up sheets, Ms. Jansen determines they will have 80 large cupcakes and 240 brownies for the bake sale. Nobody signed up to bring in cookies yet.

The students decide that they will sell the large cupcakes for $2 each, and brownies and cookies for $1 each.

  1. How much money can the students make if they sell all of the cupcakes and brownies?

    They can make 80 × $2 = $160 if they sell all of the cupcakes and 240 × $1 = $240 if they sell all of the brownies. If they sell all of both, they can make $400.

  2. How many cookies will be needed for the class to reach their goal of $500?

    The students need another $100 to reach their goal, so they need 100 cookies.

  3. How many families will need to volunteer to bring cookies, if each family brings 20 cookies?

    5 families will need to volunteer to bring in 20 cookies.

page CC 78

---

page CC 79

Part B

The bake sale will take place from 11:00 to 12:00 every school day for one week. The students will set up tables outside the school lunchroom and will invite teachers, students, and parents to the bake sale.

Ms. Jansen has decided to have 30-minute shifts for the bake sale. Two students will work at each shift.

  4. How many shifts will each of the 20 students in the class have to work during the week-long bake sale?

    There will be two shifts each day for 5 days, so 10 shifts in all. Two students will work each shift, so each student will have one shift.

page CC 79

---

page CC 80

Name _____

Performance Task 2
A Nature Hike

Part A

Colton and Rashad are hiking a trail to a waterfall in a nature preserve. After hiking for 30 minutes, they see the sign below.

You are half way there!

Rashad says, "Half-way? Is that all? That's less than $\frac{1}{3}$ of the trail."

Colton disagrees. He says, "$\frac{1}{2}$ of the trail is greater than $\frac{1}{3}$ of the trail."

  1. Who is correct? Use two different models to show whether Rashad or Colton is correct.

    Colton is correct, $\frac{1}{2}$ is greater than $\frac{1}{3}$. Check students models.

page CC 80

Colton and Rashad each have a water bottle for the hike. When they began the hike, their water bottles were full. Their water bottles are shown below.

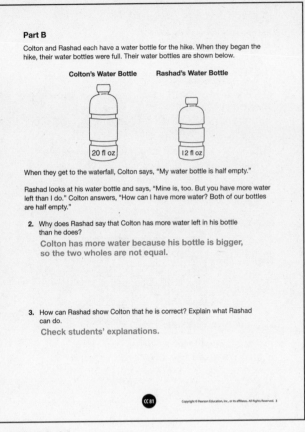

Colton's Water Bottle | **Rashad's Water Bottle**

20 fl oz | 12 fl oz

When they get to the waterfall, Colton says, "My water bottle is half empty."

Rashad looks at his water bottle and says, "Mine is, too. But you have more water left than I do." Colton answers, "How can I have more water? Both of our bottles are half empty."

2. Why does Rashad say that Colton has more water left in his bottle than he does?

Colton has more water because his bottle is bigger, so the two wholes are not equal.

3. How can Rashad show Colton that he is correct? Explain what Rashad can do.

Check students' explanations.

page CC 81

Name _____

Practice End-of-Year Assessment
Test 2

1. The picture graph shows the favorite snacks of the third grade.

Favorite Snacks of Third Grade

Food	Number of Students
Apples	☺ ☺ ☺
Carrots	☺ ☺
Crackers	☺ ☺ ☺ ☺
Peanuts	☺

Key: ☺ stands for 2 students

How many fewer students chose carrots than chose crackers?

4 students

2. a. Name a fraction equivalent to $\frac{3}{6}$.

Possible answer: $\frac{1}{2}$

b. Draw models to show why the fractions are equivalent.

Check students' models.

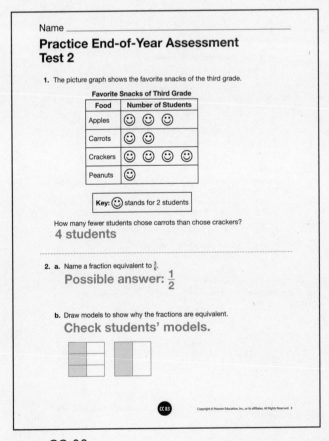

page CC 83

---

3. Abby has 2 boxes of crayons. Each box holds 8 crayons. Abby gives 6 of her crayons to her sister.

a. How many crayons does Abby have left?

10 crayons

b. Explain how you found your answer.

Possible answer: First, I multiplied 8 by 2 to find the number of crayons in the 2 boxes. Then, I subtracted 6 from 16 to find the number of crayons Abby has left.

4. Which of these numbers round to 3500 when rounded to the nearest hundred? Circle all that apply.

(3482)   3561   3550

(3450)   3409   (3490)

5. Blake makes 6 rows of stamps. Each row has 3 stamps.

a. Draw an array to show how many stamps there are in all.

Check students' arrays.

b. How many stamps are there in all?

18

page CC 84

6. Divide the number line into two equal parts. Then draw and label a point to show $\frac{1}{2}$.

7. Which multiplication facts can you use to solve the division problem?

$8 \div 2 = \boxed{}$

| $1 \times 8 = 8$ | $2 \times 2 = 4$ | $\boxed{2 \times 4 = 8}$ |
| $\boxed{4 \times 2 = 8}$ | $2 \times 8 = 16$ | $8 \times 2 = 16$ |

8. a. Draw and label a point to show $\frac{1}{6}$ on the number line.

b. Explain how you knew where to draw the point for $\frac{1}{6}$.

I used tick marks to divide the distance between 0 and 1 into 6 equal parts. Each equal part is $\frac{1}{6}$. To show $\frac{1}{6}$, I drew a point at the first tick mark to the right of 0.

page CC 85

---

9. Compare the fractions. Write >, =, or <.

$\frac{1}{6}$ $\frac{1}{3}$

Explain how you know which fraction is greater. Draw a model to support your explanation.

Check students' explanations. They should say that 1 third of a circle is larger than 1 sixth of a circle.

10. For which of these equations is 7 the missing factor? Circle all that apply.

$3 \times \boxed{} = 21$ $\boxed{} \times 5 = 30$ $\left(6 \times \boxed{} = 42\right)$

$7 \times \boxed{} = 47$ $\left(\boxed{} \times 4 = 28\right)$ $\boxed{} \times 8 = 54$

11. Look at the column for 8 in the multiplication table. What pattern do you see?

X	0	1	2	3	4	5	6	7	8
0	0	0	0	0	0	0	0	0	0
1	0	1	2	3	4	5	6	7	8
2	0	2	4	6	8	10	12	14	16
3	0	3	6	9	12	15	18	21	24
4	0	4	8	12	16	20	24	28	32
5	0	5	10	15	20	25	30	35	40
6	0	6	12	18	24	30	36	42	48
7	0	7	14	21	28	35	42	49	56
8	0	8	16	24	32	40	48	56	64

Possible answers: Each number is 8 more than the number above it. A number times 8 is always even.

page CC 86

---

12. Hal is helping his father build a wooden support for their garden. They will use 8 boards of wood that are each 4 feet long.

a. Write an equation that can be used to find how many feet of boards Hal and his father will use. Use the letter r to stand for the missing number.

Possible answer: $8 \times 4 = r$

b. How many feet of wood will they use?

32 feet

13. Leah finished her homework at 7:10. She started her homework 40 minutes earlier. At what time did Leah start her homework?

6 : 30

14. Tell how to find 3×8 by breaking apart 8 into $5 + 3$. You can use words or models.

$= (3 \times 5) + (3 \times 3) = 15 + 9 = 24$

page CC 87

---

15. Nancy is helping to clean the class fish tank. She needs to put 24 liters of water in the tank. The bucket she is using holds 4 liters. How many buckets full of water will she need to fill the tank?

6 buckets

16. Look at the numbers in the table. What pattern do you see?

5	9	13	17	21

Possible answer: Each number is 4 more than the number before it.

17. A town has 40 baseballs for its 5 baseball teams. Each team will get the same number of baseballs.

a. Write an equation to show how many baseballs each team will get. Use the letter b to stand for the missing number.

$40 \div 5 = b$

b. How many baseballs will each team get?

8 baseballs

18. What is the area of the rectangle? Be sure to use the correct units.

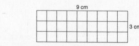

9 cm

3 cm

27 square centimeters

page CC 88

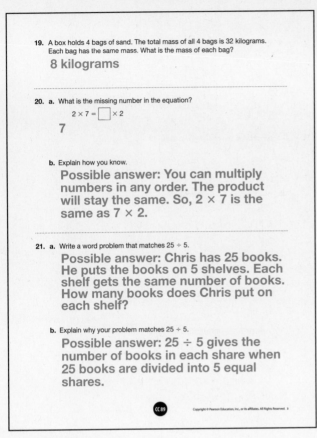

19. A box holds 4 bags of sand. The total mass of all 4 bags is 32 kilograms. Each bag has the same mass. What is the mass of each bag?

8 kilograms

20. a. What is the missing number in the equation?

$2 \times 7 = \boxed{} \times 2$

7

b. Explain how you know.

Possible answer: You can multiply numbers in any order. The product will stay the same. So, 2 × 7 is the same as 7 × 2.

21. a. Write a word problem that matches $25 \div 5$.

Possible answer: Chris has 25 books. He puts the books on 5 shelves. Each shelf gets the same number of books. How many books does Chris put on each shelf?

b. Explain why your problem matches $25 \div 5$.

Possible answer: 25 ÷ 5 gives the number of books in each share when 25 books are divided into 5 equal shares.

page CC 89

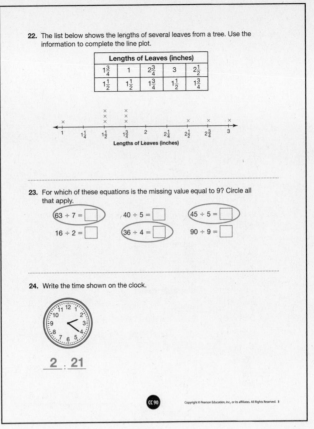

22. The list below shows the lengths of several leaves from a tree. Use the information to complete the line plot.

Lengths of Leaves (inches)				
$1\frac{3}{4}$	1	$2\frac{3}{4}$	3	$2\frac{1}{2}$
$1\frac{1}{2}$	$1\frac{1}{2}$	$1\frac{3}{4}$	$1\frac{1}{2}$	$1\frac{3}{4}$

23. For which of these equations is the missing value equal to 9? Circle all that apply.

$63 \div 7 = \boxed{}$ $40 \div 5 = \boxed{}$ $45 \div 5 = \boxed{}$

$16 \div 2 = \boxed{}$ $36 \div 4 = \boxed{}$ $90 \div 9 = \boxed{}$

24. Write the time shown on the clock.

2 : 21

page CC 90

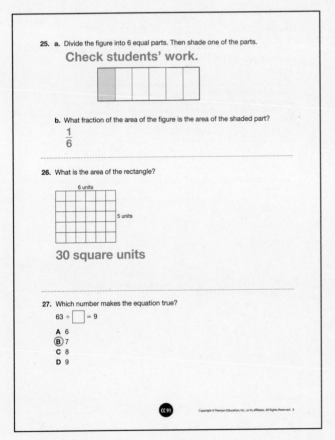

25. a. Divide the figure into 6 equal parts. Then shade one of the parts.

Check students' work.

b. What fraction of the area of the figure is the area of the shaded part?

$\frac{1}{6}$

26. What is the area of the rectangle?

6 units
5 units

30 square units

27. Which number makes the equation true?

$63 \div \boxed{} = 9$

A 6
B 7
C 8
D 9

page CC 91

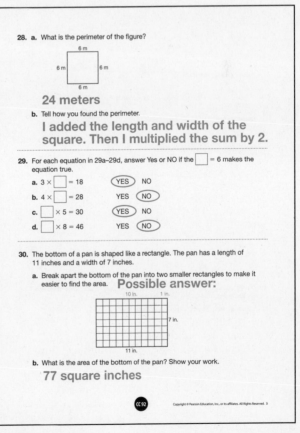

28. a. What is the perimeter of the figure?

6 m
6 m   6 m
6 m

24 meters

b. Tell how you found the perimeter.

I added the length and width of the square. Then I multiplied the sum by 2.

29. For each equation in 29a–29d, answer Yes or NO if the $\boxed{}$ = 6 makes the equation true.

a. $3 \times \boxed{} = 18$ YES   NO

b. $4 \times \boxed{} = 28$ YES   NO

c. $\boxed{} \times 5 = 30$ YES   NO

d. $\boxed{} \times 8 = 46$ YES   NO

30. The bottom of a pan is shaped like a rectangle. The pan has a length of 11 inches and a width of 7 inches.

a. Break apart the bottom of the pan into two smaller rectangles to make it easier to find the area. **Possible answer:**

10 in.   1 in.
7 in.
11 in.

b. What is the area of the bottom of the pan? Show your work.

77 square inches

page CC 92

T23

31. Explain how you can use 2 × 3 to help you find 2 × 30.

> Possible answer: I know that 2 × 3 ones is 6 ones, so 2 × 3 tens must equal 6 tens, or 60.

32. Write a multiplication fact that can help you solve the division problem.

42 ÷ 6 = ☐

7 × 6 = 42 or 6 × 7 = 42

33. A pool is shaped liked a rectangle. The length of the pool is 10 meters, and the width is 8 meters. What is the area of the pool?

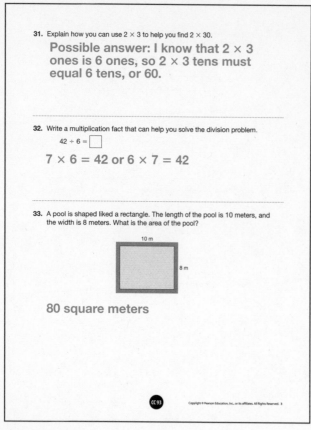

10 m

8 m

80 square meters

page CC 93

---

34. a. Divide the figure into 8 equal parts. Shade 1 of the parts.

> Possible answer:

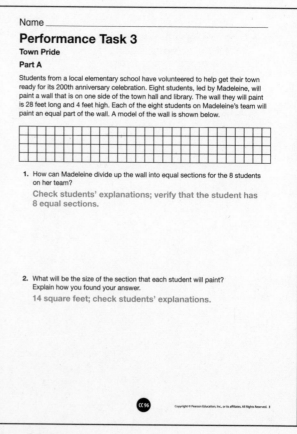

b. What fraction of the figure is shaded?

$\frac{1}{8}$

35. Which figure is not a quadrilateral?

A

Ⓒ

B

D

36. A napkin has an area of 36 square inches. Explain what this sentence means.

> Possible answer: You can completely cover the napkin with 36 unit squares. Each unit square has an area of 1 square inch and a side length of 1 inch.

page CC 94

---

37. Multiply.

8
× 8
64

38. Oliver had $14. He used some of the money to buy 5 pencils. Now Oliver has $4 left.

a. How much did each pencil cost?

$2

b. Explain how you found your answer.

> Possible answer: First, I subtracted $4 from $14 to find how much Oliver spent on pencils. Then, I divided $10 by 5 to find the cost of each pencil.

39. Add.

338
+ 457
795

40. Five friends have 35 tickets. They share the tickets equally. Hannah is one of the friends. She gives away 3 of her tickets.

a. How many tickets does Hannah have left?

4 tickets

b. Explain how you found your answer.

> Possible answer: First, I divided 35 by 5 to find how many tickets each friend gets. Then, I subtracted 3 from 7 to find how many tickets Hannah has left.

page CC 95

Name _____

Performance Task 3
Town Pride

Part A

Students from a local elementary school have volunteered to help get their town ready for its 200th anniversary celebration. Eight students, led by Madeleine, will paint a wall that is on one side of the town hall and library. The wall they will paint is 28 feet long and 4 feet high. Each of the eight students on Madeleine's team will paint an equal part of the wall. A model of the wall is shown below.

1. How can Madeleine divide up the wall into equal sections for the 8 students on her team?

Check students' explanations; verify that the student has 8 equal sections.

2. What will be the size of the section that each student will paint? Explain how you found your answer.

14 square feet; check students' explanations.

page CC 96

Part B

A second group was going to paint another wall that is 16 feet long by 4 feet high. At the last minute, the group was assigned to a different project, so Madeleine's team will paint this wall, too.

A model of the wall is shown below.

3. How can Madeleine divide up the two walls into equal sections for the 8 students in her team? (Hint: Think about whether all team members paint sections of both walls.)

Check students' explanations. Students may suggest dividing each wall into 8 equal parts or they may opt to have 5 students paint the larger wall and 3 students paint the smaller wall, with one of the three painting a small section of the larger wall

4. What is the total number of square feet each team member will paint? Explain how you know.

22 square feet; check students' explanations.

page CC 97

Performance Task 4
Paving Stones
Part A

Tami's father wants to build a patio in their back yard. The patio will be 60 inches long and 36 inches wide. He will use paving stones. He will use paving stones that are 9-inch square or paving stones that are 12 inches by 6 inches.

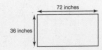

1. Which paving stone should Tami's father use if he wants to use the fewest number of paving stones? Explain your answer using models.

He should use the 9-inch paving stone, which will require 32 pacing stones. If he uses the 12-inch by 6-inch paving stone, he will need 36 stones. Check students' explanations.

page CC 98

Part B

The 9-inch square paving stones cost $3 for each paving stone. The 12-inch by 6-inch paving stones are on sale for $2 for each paving stone.

2. Which paving stone should Tami's father use if he wants to spend the least amount for the paving stones? How much will he save? Explain your answer using models or equations.

He should use the 12-inch by 6-inch paving stone. The cost for 36 of these stones is $72. The cost for 32 9-inch paving stones is $96. He will save $24. Check students' explanations.

page CC 99

Practice End-of-Year Assessments Correlation Chart
Test 1 and Test 2

The chart below provides information about the two Practice End-of-Year Assessments, Test 1, found in the students' workbook and Test 2, a secure version, found in this Teacher's Guide, starting on page CC 83. The chart lists the Standard for Mathematical Content that is the primary assessment focus of each item. It also indicates whether the standard assessed is a major, supporting or additional content emphasis (as determined by both PARCC and SBAC). The two columns on the right point to the lesson(s) in enVisionMATH Common Core and Units in Investigations where students can be directed if they need additional practice or review of concepts.

Item Test 1 and Test 2	CCSS	Content Emphasis	enVisionMATH Common Core Lessons	Investigations Units
1	3.MD.B.3	Supporting	16-3, 16-5, 16-6	U2 Inv. 1
2	3.NF.A.3	Major	10-5, 10-6	U7 Inv. 1; U7 Inv. 2
3	3.OA.D.8	Major	3-7, 5-1, 6-4, 6-7, 8-5	U3 Inv. 4
4	3.NBT.A.1	Additional	2-5	U9 Inv. 2
5	3.OA.A.3	Major	4-2, 6-2, 6-3	U5 Inv. 3
6	3.NF.A.2	Major	9-5	U7 Inv. 1
7	3.OA.B.6	Major	8-6, 8-8	U5 Inv. 4
8	3.NF.A.2	Major	9-5, 10-6	U7 Inv. 1
9	3.NF.A.3	Major	10-1, 10-2, 10-3, 10-4	U7 Inv. 1; U7 Inv. 2
10	3.OA.A.4	Major	6-2, 7-3, 8-2	U5 Inv. 4
11	3.OA.D.9	Major	2-3, 6-3	U5 Inv. 2
12	3.OA.A.3	Major	4-4, 5-1, 6-3	U5 Inv. 1; U5 Inv. 3; U6 Inv. 3
13	3.MD.A.1	Major	12-4, 12-5	U3 Inv. 3; U3 Inv. 4; U5 Inv. 1
14	3.OA.B.5	Major	5-1, 5-2, 6-1, 6-3	U5 Inv. 2; U5 Inv. 3
15	3.MD.A.2	Major	15-2	U9 Inv. 4
16	3.OA.D.9	Major	5-4, 5-5, 7-3	U5 Inv. 2
17	3.OA.A.3	Major	7-5, 8-2, 8-3	U5 Inv. 1; U5 Inv. 4; U6 Inv. 3
18	3.MD.C.6	Major	14-1, 14-4	U4 Inv. 2
19	3.MD.A.2	Major	15-3	U9 Inv. 4
20	3.OA.B.5	Major	4-3, 5-2, 6-5	U5 Inv. 2; U6 Inv. 3

Item Test 1 and Test 2	CCSS	Content Emphasis	enVisionMATH Common Core Lessons	Investigations Units
21	3.OA.A.1, 3.OA.A.2	Major	7-1, 7-2, 7-5	U5 Inv. 4
22	3.MD.B.4	Supporting	16-1, 16-2	U2 Inv. 3
23	3.OA.C.7	Major	8-3, 8-4, 8-8	U5 Inv. 4
24	3.MD.A.1	Major	12-1, 12-2	U5 Inv. 3; U5 Inv. 4; U7 Inv. 1
25	3.G.A.2	Supporting	9-1, 11-6	U7 Inv. 1; U7 Inv. 2
26	3.MD.C.6	Major	14-4	U4 Inv. 2
27	3.OA.A.4	Major	8-3, 8-4, 8-8	U5 Inv. 4
28	3.MD.D.8	Additional	13-1, 13-2, 13-3	U4 Inv. 1
29	3.OA.C.7	Major	8-4, 8-8	U6 Inv. 2; U6 Inv. 3
30	3.MD.C.7	Major	14-4, 14-5	U4 Inv. 2; U5 Inv. 3
31	3.NBT.A.3	Additional	5-5, 5-6	U5 Inv. 3
32	3.OA.B.6	Major	8-2, 8-4, 8-6	U5 Inv. 4
33	3.MD.C.7	Major	14-2, 14-3, 14-4	U5 Inv. 3
34	3.NF.A.1	Major	9-1, 9-2	U7 Inv. 1; U7 Inv. 2
35	3.G.A.1	Supporting	11-3, 11-5	U4 Inv. 3
36	3.MD.C.5	Major	14-1, 14-2	U4 Inv. 2
37	3.OA.C.7	Major	5-1, 5-2	U6 Inv. 2; U6 Inv. 3
38	3.OA.D.8	Major	8-2, 8-5, 8-6	U5 Inv. 1; U5 Inv. 4
39	3.NBT.A.2	Additional	3-7, 3-8	U1 Inv. 1; U1 Inv. 2; U8 Inv. 3
40	3.OA.D.8	Major	5-7, 6-2, 6-5, 6-9, 8-2, 8-5	U5 Inv. 1; U5 Inv. 4

Performance Tasks Scoring Rubrics

Performance Task 1 – Raising Funds

Primary Content Domains and Clusters

Operations and Algebraic Thinking: Represent and solve problems involving multiplication and division. (3.OA.A.3); Multiply and divide within 100. (3.OA.C.7); Solve problems involving the four operations, and identify and explain patterns in arithmetic. (3.OA.D.8)

Secondary Content Domains and Clusters

Measurement and Data: Solve problems involving measurement and estimation of intervals of time, liquid volumes, and masses of objects. (3.MD.A.1)

Math Practices Focus

MP 1, 2, 4, 7

Scoring Rubric

1	**Determines the amount of money to be made from the sale of all cupcakes and brownies.**	7
	Multiplies to find the amount of money to be made from the sale of all cupcakes.	
	Multiplies to find the amount of money to be made from the sale of all brownies.	
	Adds the two amounts.	
2	**Calculates the number of cookies needed to reach class goal.**	5
	Subtract amount made from the sale of cupcakes and brownies from goal.	
	Divides difference by cost of cookie.	
3	**Determines the number of families needed to volunteer to bring cookies.**	3
	Divides the number of cookies needed by 20.	
4	**Determines the number of shifts each student will have.**	5
	Finds the total number of shifts each day and for the week.	
	Multiplies to determine the number of students needed to cover all of the shifts.	
TOTAL		20

Performance Task 2 – A Nature Hike

Primary Content Domains and Clusters

Number and Operations – Fractions: Develop understanding of fractions as numbers. (3.NF.A.3.a, 3.NF.A.3.b, 3.NF.A.3.d)

Secondary Content Domains and Clusters

Measurement and Data: Solve problems involving measurement and estimation of intervals of time, liquid volumes, and masses of objects. (3.MD.A.2)

Math Practices Focus

MP 1, 2, 3, 4, 6

Scoring Rubric

1	**Fully answers the questions posed.**	5
	Identifies whose answer is correct.	
	Offers two appropriate models that match the problem situation presented.	
2	**Offers an appropriate explanation for Rashad's claim.**	5
	Recognizes that the two wholes are not equivalent.	
3	**Offers appropriate models to prove Rashad's claim.**	5
	Suggests using the same "whole" unit for both quantities.	
TOTAL		**15**

Performance Task 3 – Town Pride

Primary Content Domains and Clusters

Number and Operations – Fractions: Develop understanding of fractions as numbers. (3.NF.A.1)

Secondary Content Domains and Clusters

Measurement and Data: Geometric measurement: understand concepts of area and relate area to multiplication and addition. (3.MD.C.6, 3.MD.C.7)

Math Practices Focus

MP 1, 2, 4, 7

Scoring Rubric

1	Explains an equal division of the wall.	6
	Describes a division of the wall into 8 equal parts.	
	Explains why the division is equal.	
2	Explains how to find the size of each part.	4
	Calculates the area correctly.	
	Describes how to find the area.	
3	Explains how to divide the two walls equally.	6
	Describes a division of the two walls into 8 equal parts.	
	Explains why the division is equal.	
4	Explains how to find the size of each part.	4
	Calculates the area correctly.	
	Describes how to find the area.	
TOTAL		20

Performance Task 4 – Paving Stones

Primary Content Domains and Clusters

Measurement and Data: Geometric measurement: understand concepts of area and relate area to multiplication and addition. (3.MD.C.5, 3.MD.C.7)

Secondary Content Domains and Clusters

Operations and Algebraic Thinking: Solve problems involving the four operations, and identify and explain patterns in arithmetic. (3.OA.D.8)

Math Practices Focus

MP 1, 2, 4, 7, 8

Scoring Rubric

1	**Chooses the correct type and justifies the correct answer.**	10
	Chooses correct paving stone.	
	Explains why the square stone is the correct stone.	
	Uses models to explain answer.	
2	**Chooses the correct type, calculates savings, and justifies answers.**	10
	Uses work from part 1 to choose lower price.	
	Calculates savings correctly.	
	Justifies answers using models or equations.	
TOTAL		**20**